Kingdom Dynamics
Volume 1

Principles for Sonship

by
Dr. Ron M. Horner

Kingdom Dynamics
Volume 1

Principles for Sonship

by
Dr. Ron M. Horner

LifeSpring International Ministries
PO Box 5847
Pinehurst, North Carolina 28374
RonHorner.com

Kingdom Dynamics – Volume 1

Principles for Sonship

Copyright © 2022 Dr. Ron M. Horner

Scripture is taken from the New King James Version®. Copyright © 1982 by Thomas Nelson. Used by permission. All rights reserved. (Unless otherwise noted.)

Scripture quotations marked (TPT) are from The Passion Translation®, Copyright © 2017, 2018 by BroadStreet Publishing Group, LLC. Used by permission. All rights reserved. ThePassionTranslation.com

Scripture marked (THE MIRROR) is taken from The Mirror Study Bible by Francois du Toit. Copyright © 2021 All Rights Reserved. Used by permission of The Author.

All rights reserved. This book is protected by the copyright laws of the United States of America. This book may not be copied or reprinted for commercial gain or profit. The use of short quotations or occasional page copying for personal, or group study is permitted and encouraged. Permission will be granted upon request.

Requests for bulk sales discounts, editorial permissions, or other information should be addressed to:

LifeSpring Publishing
PO Box 5847
Pinehurst, NC 28374 USA

Additional copies available at
www.LifeSpringPublishing.com

ISBN 13 TP: 978-1-953684-33-2
ISBN 13 eBook: 978-1-953684-32-5

Cover Design by Darian Horner Design
(www.darianhorner.com)
Image: 123rf.com # 135303806

First Edition: July 2022

10 9 8 7 6 5 4 3 2

Printed in the United States of America

Table of Contents

Acknowledgements...i

Characters in this Book.......................................iii

Foreword..v

Preface..xvii

Chapter 1 The Kingdom Dynamic
   of Quantum Leaps..1

Chapter 2 The Kingdom Dynamics
   of Sonship..7

Chapter 3 The Kingdom Dynamic
   of Knowing Who You Are............................19

Chapter 4 The Kingdom Dynamic
   of the Guarantee of Heaven 23

Chapter 5 The Kingdom Dynamic
   of Trusting Your Steps 29

Chapter 6 The Kingdom Dynamics
   of Trusts..41

Chapter 7 The Kingdom Dynamics
   of Accessed Inheritance...............................63

Chapter 8 The Kingdom Dynamics
   of Transition...73

Chapter 9 The Kingdom Dynamics
   of Capture Bags 77

Chapter 10 The Kingdom Dynamics
   of the Glory & Essence of the Father........................... 83

Chapter 11 The Kingdom Dynamics
   of Plunder, Defense, & Frequencies............................. 97

Chapter 12 The Kingdom Dynamics
   of Overcoming Domains & Dominions 109

Chapter 13 The Kingdom Dynamics
   of Regained Innocence 125

Chapter 14 The Kingdom Dynamics
   of Safety & Security... 137

Chapter 15 The Kingdom Dynamics
   of Constructive Trusts... 141

Chapter 16 The Kingdom Dynamics
   of Being a Living Rainbow 147

Chapter 17 The Kingdom Dynamics
   of Co-Laboring... 155

Chapter 18 The Kingdom Dynamics
   of Governing Our Territory.. 159

Chapter 19 The Kingdom Dynamics
   of Agreement.. 171

Chapter 20 The Kingdom Dynamics
   of Knowing Our Star 181

Chapter 21 The Kingdom Dynamics
   of Obtaining Our Daily Scroll 203

Chapter 22 The Kingdom Dynamics
of Piercing the Veil of Orphanhood 213

Chapter 23 The Kingdom Dynamics
of Spiritual Authority & Governing 227

Chapter 24 The Kingdom Dynamics
of Expectancy 233

Chapter 25 The Kingdom Dynamics
of Governing from Our Star 241

Chapter 26 The Kingdom Dynamics
of Obedience 247

Chapter 27 The Kingdom Dynamics
of Engaging from Within Our Star 255

Chapter 28 The Kingdom Dynamics
of Our Arche 267

Chapter 29 The Kingdom Dynamics
of Freedom from Religion 273

Chapter 30 Living Kingdom Dynamics 283

Appendix A 287

The Kingdom Dynamic
of Accessing the Realms of Heaven 287

References 293

Description 295

About the Author 297

Other Books by Dr. Ron M. Horner 299

Acknowledgements

Heaven has been wonderfully gracious to surround me with an exceptional team who are committed to seeing the Kingdom expand upon the earth through this ministry. May Heaven's best be released to each of them and their families as we expect, extend, and expand for the Glory of the King. Thank you to all the team for all you do for the Kingdom. Special thanks to Stephanie, Anna, and Darian.

Characters in this Book

In this book you we introduced to several entities who assisted us in the writing of this book:

Adina – Ron Horner's wife

Albert – Angel who assists Sandhills Ecclesia

Ezekiel – The Chief Angel over LifeSpring

David – David Porter III is Lead Apostle of Sandhills Ecclesia and an accountant on our team

Gail – A woman in white who assists Sandhills Ecclesia

Garzan – one of Ezekiel's angelic commanders

George – A man in white who assists in the financial affairs of LifeSpring

Jason – A man in white

Joseph – A man in white

Jonathan – Angel assisting Sandhills Ecclesia

Knowledge – (Spirit of Knowledge) one of the seven spirits of God

Lydia – A woman in white who assists LifeSpring

Malcolm – A man in white who is the Headmaster of CourtsNet

Seth – A man in white who assists the Sandhills Ecclesia intercessors

Stephanie – My current Executive Assistant

Understanding (Spirit of Understanding) – one of the seven spirits of God

Wisdom (Spirit of Wisdom) – one of the seven spirits of God

Foreword

As we engaged Heaven for Sandhills Ecclesia, we could see Gail, Seth, Jonathan, and Albert. Gail and Seth were leaning against a wooden fence like you would see around a pasture. As we were to discover, the Father wanted us to deal with some things that were hindering us from activating a Kingdom Dynamic of the Father's provision. What follows is the dialogue with our heavenly assistants and the team for Sandhills Ecclesia, a church we lead (mostly via Zoom).

Gail said, "He (the Father) owns the cattle on a thousand hills."[1]

We asked, "What does Heaven have for us today?"

Gail began, "Because He owns the cattle on a thousand hills, why would we ever be concerned about what we own as His sons?"

Stephanie replied, "Well, Gail, I can tell you that in the natural we have not entirely understood this paradigm

---

[1] Psalm 50:10

of prayer or understood that we could be here as sons with the Father. We have not understood what gifts he gives us. We haven't known how or understood how to bring it down from Heaven or to have it put into our realms."

Gail asked, "Whose fault is that?"

Stephanie answered, "The churches and pastors."

Gail queried, "When and where in the Bible did it ever say to believe everything you were told by pastors or teachers? What do the prosperity preachers preach?"

Stephanie replied, "What do they preach? Name it and claim it?"

Adina added, "The wealth of the wicked is laid up for the just."

Stephanie asked, "Gail, what is it you want us to know?"

Gail leaned in close to Stephanie's face and said, "**I want you to know that all of this is y'alls!!!**"

Stephanie responded, "Okay, Gail, we've begun to learn that as sons, the Kingdom belongs to us as His children, that the King always gives to the sons. In this respect, knowing that all of this belongs to us and that He owns "the cattle on a thousand hills," are you talking to us specifically about prosperity or provision?"

It was **provision** that she was talking about.

Gail said, "*'Seek first the Kingdom of God...and **all these things** (waving her hands at the cattle on the hills) will be added unto you.'*"[2] Then she did it again by waving her hand and showing the Kingdom, showing the cattle on a thousand Hills, showing the provision that He has. **"You've dropped the ball as Christians."**

David added, "We have thrown the baby out with the bath water."

Gail remarked, "It is the whole thing of 'not to worry about tomorrow, what we shall eat or drink, what clothes we shall wear'[3] but to recognize, **the provision is already there**. It has *been* provided."

> "*Grace and peace be multiplied to you in the knowledge of God and of Jesus our Lord, ³ as His divine power has given to us **all things that pertain to life and G0000odliness**, through **the knowledge** of Him who called us by glory and virtue, ⁴ by which have been given to us exceedingly great and precious promises, that through these you may be partakers of the divine nature, having escaped the corruption that is in the world through lust.*" (2 Peter 1:2-3)

Stephanie commented, "This is about people realizing that the time that we're in with markets crashing, inflation going through the roof, the gasoline prices are crazy, and people are worried about their jobs and their

---

[2] Matthew 6:33
[3] Matthew 6:25-34

ability to pay for groceries. That's not what we are supposed to do. We are His kids. Gail, what are the next steps?"

Next Steps

Gail replied, "You step in! Step *into* Heaven. You're doing the generational work. You're cleaning up the lineages. He *owns* the cattle on a thousand hills. *It's yours. Take it.* Believe. Trust Him. It *doesn't matter what the world looks like.* Turn all of that off." (She was talking about the frequencies.)

Corporately Step In:

David interjected, "The provision that you feel like you are lacking when you're a Kingdom kid is a lie. You are **a son**. There is **no** lack. Take Heaven's provision. Have your angels bring it into your realms.

"Sunday, *supernatural transactions* are going to be happening."

We then commissioned Jonathan and Albert by saying,

> *We commission you, in time and out of time,[4] to go ahead of time, preparing the way, for the provision that the Father has for 'the cattle on the*

---

[4] See the book *Commissioning Angels* for further discussion of this phrase.

thousand hills' for the people, for the understanding and the knowledge that's going to be present, for Wisdom, who's going to be there, and for the revelation to be brought into the earth realm—to be pulled down for the Kingdom kids to get the provision they need in the moment. The 'in time' miracles—the signs and the wonders—go ahead of time bringing them, preparing the way.

We commission you to the full use of the tools that you have. We commission you to co-labor with all of the other angels—Ezekiel, his commanders, and his ranks.

It is 'manna from Heaven,' but this isn't the kind of manna that at the end of the day, we've got to discard. This isn't that kind of manna. This is the tangible manna coming.

We commission you to the signs and wonders and to bring it to bear. We commission you to trumpet the visions that the people will see, to trumpet the sounds that they will hear, and to bring in the spoils, the spoils from the plundering, in Jesus mighty name.

Gail was now on a horse, and she said, "Let's ride! Have them feel the wind at their face, the very breath of God, God breathed, God ordained manna, desire sensory overload!"

Stephanie exclaimed, "Heaven is rejoicing, rejoice people! *Rejoice sons of the Most High!*

Gail and her horse disappeared over a hilltop, but Seth was still present. He said, "Dynamics. That's what this is, Kingdom Dynamics."

Dispel Fear

David added, "What I've been getting is we are to **dispel fear as it relates to prosperity,** even the preaching of the prosperity doctrine. Many have 'thrown the baby out with the bath water' because of teachings that we have heard. Even people who have been affected by what we have coined as a prosperity gospel, and *we have, out of ignorance, shunned this revelation—this truth.*

"As you were talking Stephanie, I was seeing Gail against the fence, and I heard when you were saying, 'This is for us, this is our inheritance,' so as a result of that shunning of this truth, *we have played it safe.* Many in the Body of Christ have played it safe because we didn't want to be a part of that movement or thrown in that melting pot if you will. We just didn't touch it. But **regarding the cattle on a thousand hills, I heard 'this is real estate—this is Heaven's real estate.'** *This is part of Heaven's real estate. It's part of what belongs to us*, but *if we don't believe that we can receive it, then it'll stay just as it is.* But that's what I'm sensing. Gail is trying to get the message out to us. **Father wants to bless us tremendously.** You said something that was key, 'This manna is not the kind of manna that's going to be discarded.' It's going to be not just something that's going to come and go. This is God's intent for us."

David continued, "I saw, while you were talking, the cover of Dr. Ron's book, *Your Wages Have a Voice*. I sense that there is a resurgence of that revelation that Heaven wants to release in this time. I know Dr. Ron said it was written 15 years ago and was his very first book. And perhaps the body was not ready for it, and Sandhills wasn't here. So now that Sandhills Ecclesia is here, I am sensing that God is doing something with that book, with the revelation that he gave you, Dr. Ron, many years ago. It is positioning us. *Some of us who are not in position are going to be positioned, some who were in position and pulled out of position, will be repositioned.*

"I keep hearing that *out of fear* many said, '**I don't want to be a part of the prosperity group.**' Well, there is still truth, and in *every element of what we find, what people turn into a joke, often begins with truth.*"

Court Case

We had been made aware of a court case we are to bring for the body.

1. First of all, we are to **repent regarding the prosperity preachers in general**. Heaven told us recently, there is truth in it. But when you put any element of non-truth, the whole thing becomes a lie.

2. The second thing is, we are to **repent on behalf of those of us who accused those preachers**. They don't need any other accusations on them. They have enough false verdicts on them, they don't need us doing that.
3. The other thing is we are to **repent for those who didn't use discernment and got hurt by the said 'prosperity preachers'**—for sending money their way, thinking we were going to get something in return. Some preachers used manipulative witchcraft. It's like charismatic witchcraft, both ways. The prosperity preachers used it, and those that sowed into their ministries used it because it was for the sake of getting and not giving.
4. We are to repent **for those who ended up not believing at all**, who didn't believe and don't believe that they have treasures in and from Heaven. We are to repent **for their unbelief** that they really cannot get that now, that they think it's only for the future, when they're in Heaven. That is where they/we 'threw the baby out with the bath water'
5. We are to **repent about not following and seeking Heaven,** because it's <u>not about following the prosperity teaching</u>. *It's about seeking the Father for what He has.* It's part of that relational building. When we step into Heaven, and we seek His face, and we seek His Kingdom, we ask Him what He has for us. *It's*

a relational time for the saints to say, 'Heaven, what do you have for me today?' And Him saying, 'Well, I have a thousand cattle on a thousand Hills to give you right now.' That's relational.

I recently had a conversation with David, one of our team members about the wealth and the depth regarding Matthew 6:33. I said Matthew 6:33 deals with provision, but it does not necessarily deal with abundance.

Sons must become comfortable in who they are and what they possess in the Father.

The purpose of sonship is to establish the covenant, to establish His Kingdom. Scripturally, Proverbs 6:23 is what we present to the body:

> *[23] For truth is a bright beam of light shining into every area of your life instructing and correcting you to discover the ways to Godly living. (TPT)*

That's what this paradigm has brought to the body. That's the scripture. The specific word is about listening to your parents or listening to those that are fatherly figures, motherly figures, and what that wisdom brings to you. That's the whole concept around that proverb, but that's the one that was highlighted to me.

> *[20] My son obey your father's Godly instruction and follow your mother's life giving teaching, fill your*

heart with their advice and let your life be shaped by what they've taught you. (TPT)

²²And I will whisper to you at every sunrise and direct you through a brand new day. Their wisdom will guide you wherever you go and keep you from bringing harm to yourself. (TPT)

God is redeeming the time and restoring what the cankerworm, the palmerworm, and the caterpillar have destroyed with interest—with interest!

Heaven, thank you for this revelation. We thank you for what you're going to do in people's lives.

We thank You, Father, that You're constantly telling your sons who they are and the provision You have for them and that You want this relationship with them. They don't have to worry about tomorrow. We don't have to worry about tomorrow. We can just step in, literally step into Heaven, and receive. Thank You, Father. Thank You, Jesus.

The court case was specifically about **repentance for the wrong preaching of Heaven's prosperity.**

Because some incorporated the lie as part of the truth, we should not throw the baby out with the bath water. Some fed their own greed and lusted for material things. *There was original truth about the preaching that the enemy hijacked.*

Prosper and be in health, it is part of the packet of being a son of God. However, there's wisdom and revelation and knowledge that goes with handling wealth.

—Gail, Seth, Jonathan,
Albert, and the Sandhills
Ecclesia Team

Preface

A few months ago, a man in white known as Malcolm began to teach Stephanie and me on various topics that he referred to as Kingdom Dynamics. Kingdom Dynamics are principles and insights into strategies, tools, resources and more that are available to the sons Heaven is bringing forth.

The term 'son' is a positional term, not gender related when in use in this book. We have been given access to things that will help us as we mature in our walk with the Father. Dr. Sam Soleyn wrote about the stages of sonship in his book, "The Elementary Doctrines." I will summarize this material to help you understand where you have been, where you are, and where you are going in your journey with the Father.

The foundation of this journey is the Father-Son relationship, with the result being a Holy Nation that functions as one body under the headship of Jesus. That will demonstrate the Kingdom of God upon the earth.

The initial stage is, of course, being a newborn child or newly born-again believer. We are baptized (immersed) into the Body of Christ by Holy Spirit (1 Corinthians 12:13). Our role in this is simply our surrender to the work of Holy Spirit to convict us and convince us. When you are first born-again you are an heir of the provision and promises of God. You are a *nēpios*,[5] a babe or small child not yet able to speak. A *nēpios* is like an heir under guardianship. Such a one is not mature enough or trained sufficiently to have free access to the resources of the household. They are only ready to drink milk spiritually. They are certainly not ready to drive the family car! The starting place for the *nēpios* is the elementary doctrines of Hebrews 6:1-3.

The second stage is the *paidion*[6] stage, often translated in Scripture as a small—in essence, a toddler.

> *I write to you, fathers, Because you have known Him who is from the beginning. I write to you, young men, Because you have overcome the wicked one. I write to you, **little children**, Because you have known the Father. (1 John 2:13) (Emphasis mine)*

A child at this stage can recognize the Father, but a lack of depth remains in the relationship.

---

[5] Galatians 4:1, see Strong's #3516
[6] Strong's #3818

The third stage is the *teknon*[7]—where the son has sufficient maturity to be given opportunity and responsibility to respond to rulership and discipline.

I write to you, little children, Because your sins are forgiven you for His name's sake. (1 John 2:12)

This is the stage mentioned in John 1:12, which is familiar to most of us:

*But as many as received Him, to them He gave the right to become **children** of God, to those who believe in His name... (John 1:12) (Emphasis mine)*

A son at this stage can engage in a relationship with heavenly Father. In Matthew 21:28-31, Jesus shares a parable regarding the man with two sons. One he instructed to go work in his vineyard and the son said he would, but then did not. The second son had the same behavior. The difference was that the first son, after ignoring his father's instruction regretted not going and then went and worked in the vineyard. Jesus asked the question of the listeners to this parable, "Which one did the will of his father?" The rebellion each son demonstrated simply exposed that more training was necessary for both.

The fourth stage is *neaniskos*[8] stage where John describes one at this stage as a young man.

---

[7] Strong's G5040
[8] Strong's G3495

> *¹² I write to you, fathers, Because you have known Him who is from the beginning. I write to you, young men, Because you have overcome the wicked one. I write to you, little children, Because you have known the Father. ¹³ I have written to you, fathers, Because you have known Him who is from the beginning. I have written to you, **young men**, Because you are strong, and the word of God abides in you, And you have overcome the wicked one. (1 John 2:14) (Emphasis mine)*

The son at this stage has several things going for him:

- He is strong
- He has the Word of God abiding in him
- He has overcome the wicked one
- He can take on some responsibility

All these are great characteristics, but still the son has not reached the place he needs to reach. This son has been tested, displayed strength, and utilized the Word of God. He has been able to endure suffering and been refined in the process.

The final stage, however, is where you want to be. This is known in Greek as becoming a *uihos*[9] son (pronounces "wee-os"). This is the son who can fully represent the Father. In Jewish culture, a son served as an apprentice to his father through his teen years and through his twenties with the goal being that upon reaching the age of thirty, he would be fully vested and

---

[9] Strong's G5207

be able to assume the father's business, acting on behalf of the father with all the rights and privileges of the father.

You may have wondered why Jesus waited until he was thirty years of age to begin his ministry. It was to fulfill Jewish custom. At thirty, he was qualified to take over the family business. Remember, he began training for the "Father's business" at age twelve, when he was found among the teachers of the law in the temple.

The parable Jesus taught of the man who owned a vineyard[10] and sent servants to collect the rent uses this word for son. The vine-growers, when they saw the servant, killed him. This happened multiple times. Finally, the father says, 'I will send my *uihos* son. Surely, they will respect him, but they did not and killed him as well.

The *uihos* carries a measure of the Glory of God wherever he is sent. He establishes the righteousness of the Father wherever he goes. He is a fully mature son. That is the desire of the Father for each of us. The Kingdom Dynamics shared with us by Malcolm and others will enrich your life as we progress in our journey of sonship.

The progression through these stages can be swift or slow. It depends on your willingness to cooperate with

---

[10] Matthew 21:33-44

Heaven. What has taken me years to learn and embrace, I hope will only take you months or a few short years.

Surrender is a key aspect.

---

*We must be willing to surrender
who we think we are
and embrace who and what
the Father says concerning us.*

A resource that will help you is the small book by Harold Eberle entitled *Precious in His Sight*.[11] Most of us were raised with the mentality that we are sinners by nature, and we will never be much more than a worm. That is not what Heaven says about you. The misconception that we are just worms came from a bad translation of Scripture embraced by Augustine, an early church Father. The problem with that line of thinking is that, when your foundation is wrong, you can't possibly build right from that point forward.

In the area I live in, we have very sandy soil. A church in the area was building a new facility and instead of building a footer for the foundation that needed to be three feet deep, they opted to "save money" and only dug the footer to be two feet deep. It did not take but a short while once the building was completed for the building to begin settling on that insufficient foundation. The

---

[11] https://www.worldcastministries.com/store/p10/Precious_in_His_Sight.html

walls began to crack, the doors became misaligned and would not open or close correctly, and other issues developed along the way. The problem was, due to the size of the building, no practical solution could be accomplished. A bad foundation made all the difference.

The principle is true in our own lives. You must have a solid foundation of truth to build your life upon. You are a son and sons of the king sit at the king's table.

We must be willing to admit some of the things, in fact MANY of the things we have been taught, were wrong. We need new understandings in a myriad of ways. Where Heaven wants to take us will necessitate our willingness to surrender the old and embrace the new. May we be willing to go through that process—all the way. This book includes many of those things we either need to embrace or we need to utilize.

Some of the chapters are included in other recent books but are included here because they specifically were a part of the Kingdom Dynamics taught us by Heaven. If you have read one of these chapters in another book, I encourage you to not skip it in this book because I have modified or enhanced the material in this book from other books as more insight and revelation came. Begin to access and exercise the various Kingdom Dynamics and watch—not only your life change—but the lives of those around you.

As you begin to read, instruct your soul to step back and call your spirit forward, also, call your angels near and commission them to assist you in the reception of the revelation contained in this book. Instruct your soul to be a bridge from your spirit to your body, and not to be a gatekeeper hindering the flow of revelation. Commission the angels to prepare your environment and make it conducive to reading with your spirit engaged. Have fun!

———·———

Chapter 1
The Kingdom Dynamic of Quantum Leaps

As Stephanie and I engaged Heaven this day, Malcolm joined us and asked if we would like to know about "quantum leaps," which he referred to as "Heaven's math."

He remarked that it was a leap forward—a projection.[12] The way he showed it to us was a projection of someone in *one* space, then projecting their thought, and then they were in *another* space.

In our realm, there are rules to time and space. In Heaven, there are no rules to time and space. We are already quantum leaping when we step into Heaven because there is no time or space in Heaven.

---

[12] Malcolm is not speaking of the occult practice of astral projection which is a projection of the soul into another space.

We were asked to consider, *"Are we in the future?"* What are we really discussing? These are future ideas. These come from future spaces. These are future concepts. That is what Heaven is—it's quantum. It's forward thinking, It's future dynamics. It's Kingdom principles.

Laying Down

We have been walking in quantum dynamics, every day, through this revelation of stepping into Heaven.[13] When we say we are stepping into Heaven, it is a stepping up—higher, dimensionally. It is a projection. To understand this, we must lay aside the objects of our affection, which is flesh. We are not talking about literally laying your flesh down as in death, but quantum physics is life. It can be done IN life, outside of the constraints of time and space. Let's take a minute to take that into our soul.[14]

---

[13] The revelation of the simplicity of stepping into Heaven, see *"The Kingdom Dynamic of Accessing the Realms of Heaven"* in the Appendix.

[14] Colossians 3:1-2 *"See yourselves co-raised with Christ! Now ponder with persuasion the consequence of your co-inclusion in him. Relocate yourselves mentally! Engage your thoughts with throne room realities where you are co-seated with Christ in the executive authority of God's right hand. ² Becoming affectionately acquainted with throne room thoughts will keep you from being distracted again by the earthly [soul-ruled] realm."* du Toit, Francois. *Mirror Study Bible* (p. 750). Kindle Edition.

We just haven't packaged it in this language. When we step into heaven, we are stepping from one realm into an entirely different realm.

When we were kids, we were taught that Heaven was somewhere beyond the stars, but it is as close as our nose—or closer. Jesus said, "The Kingdom of Heaven is at hand."[15]

If you could say at this point that your mind is officially blown, Heaven wants you to know that is a specialty of theirs.

Think of it this way. We are quantumly stepping into Heaven to have court discussions and heavenly experiences. **Have we thought about the fact that there is something past even that—that as sons, we can be ruling and reigning *in* other dimensions, *from* other dimensions on behalf of the Kingdom as sons?** Now that's a quantum shakeup for our minds.

Yes, Malcolm was talking about us—as sons, ruling and reigning beyond just what we consider the heavenly realms.[16] Heaven is so much bigger that what we have thought.

---

[15] Matthew 4:17
[16] This is discussed in my book, *Engaging Heaven for Trade*, LifeSpring Publishing (2022).

Heaven told us one time that there are 12 Heavens. We are only dealing with the first one or two—and there are 33 dimensions.[17]

Know that Satan stole that for the 33 degrees of Freemasonry. He's trying to copycat. He can't create, so he's got to cheat and steal. We are only learning from this first realm of Heaven. What information do you think is in the next?

Other Dimensions

Malcolm, as our heavenly tutor, was explaining that we can rule and reign *in* other dimensions *from* those dimensions while still here. That's why we lay our body down, so our spirit can go where it needs to go. We practice it every night when we go to sleep. I release my spirit to Heaven to go check in with my calendar in Heaven and do what's on the calendar during the night. I can release my spirit to go wherever the Father wants it to go, which could be another dimension, to rule and reign in that dimension.

There was a television show in the eighties that began to introduce us to this, with the actor Scott Bakula called *Quantum Leap*. His character Sam would quantum leap from one place to the another, yet he never knew when he was going leap or where or where he would end up.

---

[17] Ibid.

Paradigms of Thought

Paradigms of thought are where quantum leaps will be able to be manifest.

*The sons must know
they are sons in order to son.*

This isn't breaking rules. This isn't even challenging scientific implications of the past concerning them. Father has laid little bits and pieces of this in some men's hearts for a long time. They knew principles, they knew equations, but they didn't know the way rulership is earned as sons and as rulers. It will be handed down from these heavenly places.

*There is a fine line between
sonship and kingship.*

Sonship requires faith of *who* they are, *whose* they are and *that* they are—meaning sons. Kingship, especially in the natural, comes down a lineage. While our lineage is in Jesus, our sonship is from the Father. There are no allotments of misusage in this place. That is why it is earned. It's trusted. In other words, we are trusted by the Father, and its authority is quantifiable. These are the next steps.

Chapter 2
The Kingdom Dynamics of Sonship

Our spirit has an identity of quantitative born-againness,[18] as well as a recognition of its position in Heaven, and complete acceptance of sonship. Our spirit should operate in these things with increasing revelation, knowledge, understanding, grasp, and stance. By gaining these things, our spiritual stature will increase. As it does, our spirit will translate that to our soul.

We must keep moving in Kingdom—living from the Kingdom that is within us. It is another way to say spirit-forward. We know how people say, "I receive that." What if they were saying, *"I welcome that spirit seed of blessing into my spirit realm. I welcome it into my realm, and I assign angels to water that in my realm."* That is like

---

[18] Yes, that is how Heaven said it to us.

tending the garden of our spirit man with the help of angels who operate in that dimension.

The words of our mouth are *typically controlled* by our soul, but that is not the way it is meant to be.

A redeemed son maturing in sonship should have his words from his spirit.

If the whole church, the Bride of Christ, had all their words come *from their spirit*, it would change a great many things.

A confrontation would become an edification because the flow of revelation is in the spirit.

This is part of the increasing understanding and maturing of the saints. They are getting stronger in this. We *are* getting stronger in this, but we have work to do.

The Revelation of Sonship

The revelation of sonship is in direct correlation with the revelation of our identity as a son of God, not a son who does the work of the Father's kingdom, but the son who is loved unconditionally by the Father.

Remember the story of the prodigal son in scripture. We are so much more than we think we are. The Father's good pleasure is to begin to release the Spirit of God to give courage to those willing to risk living from their spirit in this manner. A lot of humanity will miss this. This does not grieve the Father, but it is not the full measure of His blessing toward humanity through Christ.

Living from the soul alone is not a sin, but neither is it the full plan of God for this generation and future generations. This is what religious tradition, religious teaching, and religiosity through ritual and tradition have tried to squelch, for these are not of the Kingdom of your Father. More and more, religious tradition has blinded people from the reality of hell.

The Coming Power Surge

Holy Spirit says there is a *power surge* coming to the earth. There is a power surge coming into the Bride. Not all will choose to walk in the power surge because many will be overwhelmed, just as a power surge short circuits the wiring in many houses.

A power surge is coming to the bride to continue the process of her growth and to display the splendors of God to His chosen sons and daughters.

As we have received His love and His acceptance through Jesus, the Son, this power surge will sway tall buildings like a jack hammer. It will seem to shake the ground upon which our feet walk. It will bring down ten-story buildings made by man, figuratively speaking. It will reduce the rebellious arguments of the world, the arguments of worldliness. It will set aflame a new direction in the church of Jesus Christ regarding how the church has access to the realms of the Kingdom of God and their invitation to that realm.

Once we truly grasp the message of the resurrection as described by Paul in Romans 4, we will be forever changed. The Mirror Translation describes it wonderfully:

> [24]*Scripture was written with us in mind! The same conclusion is now equally relevant in our realizing the significance of Jesus' resurrection from the dead.*
>
> [25] *Our sins resulted in His death; His resurrection is* ***proof of our righteousness****. Here is the equation: He was handed over because of our short fallings [our fallen mindset]; He was raised because we were declared righteous! His resurrection is the official receipt to our acquittal. (THE MIRROR)*

A few verses before, Paul wrote in Romans 4:

> [7] *Oh what happy progress one makes with the weight of sin and guilt removed and one's slate wiped clean!* [8] *How blessed is the one who receives a receipt instead of an invoice for their sins. (THE MIRROR)*

We forget that when man was created, God looked at him and deemed what He had made as "very good." We have sinned, but our original design was that we would not miss the mark, that we would not operate outside of the original blueprint of our design. As Heaven taught us, we were once (before our coming to earth) in a meeting with Father, Jesus, and Holy Spirit. They showed us their plans for our life, and we accepted. We then simply waited until it was time for our conception on the earth. We were born and began to live our life. Environmental factors and influences affected our lives, our beliefs, our expectations, and sin entered the picture. Each sin was simply designed to divert us from the Father's plan for us, to keep us from fulfilling our personal destiny scroll.

An Original Blueprint

The Father had an original blueprint for us laid out before the foundation of the world. Peter described it this way:

> *[1] I am Simon the Rock, bondman, and ambassador of Jesus Christ. We are in this together; God's faith sees **everyone equally valued** and justified in Jesus Christ our Savior. [2] God's desire is that we may now increasingly be overwhelmed with grace as His divine influence within us and become fully acquainted with the awareness of our oneness. The way He has always known us is realized in Jesus our Master. [3] By **His divine engineering He gifted us with all that it takes to live life to***

the full, *where our ordinary day to day lives mirror our devotion and romance with our Maker.* ***His intimate knowledge of us introduces us to ourselves again and elevates us to a position where His original intention is clearly perceived!***

*⁴ This is exactly what **God always had in mind** for us; every one of His abundant and priceless promises pointed to **our restored participation in our Godly origin! This is His gift to us!** In this fellowship we have escaped the distorted influence of the corrupt cosmic virus of greed. (2 Peter 1:1-4 THE MIRROR) (Emphasis mine)*

Perhaps we are more familiar with this rendering of verses 3-4:

*³ As His divine power has given to us **all things that pertain to life and godliness**, through the knowledge of Him who called us by glory and virtue, ⁴ by which have been given to us exceedingly great and precious promises, that through these **you may be partakers of the divine nature**, having escaped the corruption that is in the world through lust. (2 Peter 1:3-4)*

However, the "knowledge of Him" in verse 3 is not our knowledge of the Father, but of His knowledge of us. He has had knowledge of us far longer than we have of Him. Remember Jeremiah 1:5 where He knew Jeremiah before he was formed in his mother's womb.

In essence, we have been re-booted to the original settings. The Father has done all that is necessary to restore us to our original design. He has even given us His faith to believe this with. Our responsibility is to yield to the Father in this process and live out of His viewpoint of us instead of our own viewpoint of ourselves.

Comprehending Who We Are

Paul, the Apostle expressed this in Romans 12:1-3:

*¹ Live consistent with who you really are, inspired by the loving kindness of God. My brothers, the most practical expression of worship is to **make your bodies available to Him as a living sacrifice;** this pleases Him more than any religious routine. **He desires to find visible, individual expression in your person.***

*² Do not allow current religious tradition to mold you into its pattern of reasoning. Like an inspired artist, give attention to the detail of God's desire to find expression in you. **Become acquainted with perfection.** To accommodate yourself to the delight and good pleasure of Him will transform your thoughts afresh from within.*

*³ His grace gift inspires me to say to you that your thinking must be consistent with everything that is within you according to the measure of **faith that God has apportioned** to every individual.*

> ***Let the revelation of redemption shape your thoughts.*** *(THE MIRROR) (Emphasis mine)*

He designed for each of us to become sons and provided all we need to live from that location.

When we comprehend <u>whose</u> we are it will be easier to accept <u>who</u> we are.

Peter had much more to say about how to come to the realization of this new way of life in 2 Peter chapter 1:

> ⁵ *Now [in the light of what we are gifted with in Christ], the stage is set to display life's excellence. Explore the adventures of faith! Imagine the extreme dedication and focus of a conductor of music; how he would diligently acquaint himself with every individual voice in the choir, as well as the contribution of every specific instrument, to follow the precise sound represented in every single note to give maximum credit to the original composition.* ***This is exactly what it means to exhibit the divine character. You are the choir conductor of your own life.*** *Familiarize yourselves with every ingredient that faith unfolds!* ***See there how elevated you are,*** *and* ***from within this position [of your co-seatedness in Christ], enlightened perspective will dawn within you.*** ⁶ *Here you will realize your inner strength and how fully competent you are to prevail in patient perseverance amid any contradiction.* ***It is from***

within this place of enlightened perspective that meaningful devotion and worship ignite! *(Spiritual strength exceeds mind-, muscle- or willpower by far!)*

⁷ In worship you will find a genuine fondness for others. At the heart of everything that faith unfolds is the agape love of God. ⁸ While you diligently rehearse the exact qualities of every divine attribute within you; the volume will rise with ever increasing gusto, guarding you from being ineffective and barren in your knowledge of the Christ-life, displayed with such authority and eloquence in Jesus. If anyone feels that these things are absent in his life, they are not; **spiritual blindness and short-sightedness only veil them from you. This happens when one loses sight of one's innocence.**

¹⁰ Therefore I would encourage you my fellow family, to make every immediate effort to **become cemented in the knowledge of our original identity revealed and confirmed in the logic of God.** *Fully engage these realities in your lifestyle, and so you will never fail. ¹¹ Thus the great Conductor of music will draw your life into the full volume of the harmony of the ages, the royal song of our Savior Jesus Christ.*

¹² Having said all this I am sure that you can appreciate why I feel so urgent in my commitment to you to repeatedly bring these things to your attention as indeed you have already taken your *stand for the truth as it is now revealed. ¹³ So while I am still in this body-suit, I take my lead from the **revelation of righteousness** and make it my business to thoroughly stir you until these truths become permanently molded in your memory. (2 Peter 1: 5-13 THE MIRROR) (Emphasis mine)*

Peter had comprehended these truths about the plan of God, as had others of the early followers of Jesus, including John, who had this to add to the narrative:

*¹ The Logos is the source; **everything commences in Him.** The initial reports concerning Him that have reached our ears, and which we indeed bore witness to with our own eyes—to the point that we became irresistibly attracted—now captivates our gaze. In Him we witnessed tangible life in its most articulate form.*

*² **The same life** that was face to face with the Father from the beginning, **has now dawned on us!** The infinite life of the Father became visible before our eyes in a human person!*

*³ We include you in this conversation; **you are the immediate audience of the logic of God!** This is the Word that always was; we saw Him incarnate and witnessed His language as defining our lives. **In the incarnation Jesus includes mankind in the eternal friendship of the Father and the Son!** This life now finds expression in an unreserved union.*

⁷ We are invited to explore the dimensions of the same light that engulfs God; **when we see the light in His light, fellowship ignites!** *In His light we understand* **how the blood of Jesus Christ is the removal of every stain of sin! The success of the cross celebrates our redeemed innocence!**

⁸ To claim innocence by our own efforts under the law of personal performance is to deceive ourselves and to deliberately ignore the truth. The truth about you **does not mean that you now have to go into denial if you have done something wrong!**

⁹ **When we communicate what God says about our sins, we discover what He believes concerning our redeemed oneness and innocence!** *We are* **cleansed from every distortion we believed about ourselves!** *Likeness is redeemed! (THE MIRROR) (Emphasis mine)*

I recognize that I have used a lot of Scriptures from the Mirror Translation. The reason is that Francois du Toit has grasped the expression of sonship in the Scriptures better than any translation of the New Testament that I am aware of. Many of the translations that are available reinforce the traditional concept of the sin nature and how we are fallen creatures hardly worth saving. Such is not the case. The Father has had a plan for each of us all along. He never stopped believing that plan for us and was always working us around to get back on track where we might have strayed.

If we see ourselves as He sees us, we will *be* different because we ARE different! Let's begin to live out of that difference. Creation awaits your unveiling.[19]

———— · ————

---

[19] Romans 8:19

Chapter 3

The Kingdom Dynamic of Knowing Who You Are

Heaven enjoys celebrating its sons. As a matter of fact, Heaven celebrates *over* its sons in what would we consider in our time, *every day,* because there is no day or night in Heaven. It is continual.

Picture the Father walking through the streets of Heaven. Picture small cafes—very casual eating places, that people in the natural would go to. See what we would think of as storefronts and the Father walking down the street and He's going, "Hey, did you see my son David today!" He was celebrating David (with everyone there). "Did you see my son Adina today!" And celebrating Adina. "Did you see my son Stephanie today!" Heaven is always celebrating its sons.

Clearing the Misconception

There is a misconception of how the Father views His sons, that He's sitting on this pious throne, looking through a book, making judgments on things like, "Oh, David didn't quite make it the way David needed to make it today." That is a huge lie and a misconception. The Father *continually* celebrates His sons. We need to remember that it is because *of* Jesus and His death on the cross and the finality of that. **The sons need to know the Father only sees them as completely righteous, completely clean, and able to come to stand boldly for before Him *AS* a son.**

Just as your sons would ask for the simplistic thing like, 'Hey Dad, can I have the keys to the car?' Well, as a father, you would give that freely—well to *most* sons we would give the keys to the car.

This is confirmed in 2 Corinthians 5:21:

This is the divine exchange: He who knew no sin (Jesus) embraced our distortion; He appeared to be without form; this was the mystery of God's prophetic poetry. ***He was disguised in our distorted image*** *and* ***marred with our iniquities;*** *He* ***took our sorrows, our pain, and our shame to His grave*** *and* ***birthed His righteousness in us.*** *He* ***took our sins*** *and we* ***became His innocence.*** *(THE MIRROR) (Emphasis mine)*

If only we could know the joy the Father has *in each one of us in His heart, upon His lips*—as His sons. We are His sons—sons of the Most High.

The LORD your God in your midst, The Mighty One, will save; He will rejoice over you with gladness, He will quiet you with His love, **He will rejoice over you with singing.** *(Zephaniah 3:17) (Emphasis added)*

We often do get caught up in how we've made a mistake that day and how God must be feeling about us, but that is a lie from the pit of hell. It is a misdirection from Satan because he knows **once the sons know who they are in their sonship, the gates of hell surely will not prevail.**

Shaking the Gates of Hell

Every son is on the same level.

We are in this together; God's faith sees everyone **equally valued** *and* **justified in Jesus Christ** *our Savior. (2 Peter 1:1 THE MIRROR) (Emphasis added)*

---

*Knowing who we are as a son
and knowing that we are a son
shakes the very gates of hell.
They won't prevail.*

Every son has **the same access** to the Father, **the same level** to the Father, **the same joy the Father has** for every son, **the same celebration**, uniquely to who we are. **Sonship puts us *all* on an even plane.** Satan has tried to steal the idea of sonship from the sons, and we are taking it back *through* the Son.

We are in fact celebrated. We have the same access to the Father. I don't have a level of access to the Father that you do not also possess. Let's simply step into the access that is ours and enjoy being a son.

———·———

Chapter 4

The Kingdom Dynamic of the Guarantee of Heaven

Today's engagement opened with a reminder to those near the ministry to use the curtains and the veils.[20] We need to view it and think of it as strategy. We immediately requested of the Father curtains and veils for Ezekiel, his commanders, and ranks and commissioned him to their use for the ministry and the families of those involved in LifeSpring. Immediately, we saw two huge shields came up behind Ezekiel, like they were wings, but they were shields.

Ezekiel reminded us that a lot of angst was going on in the spirit realm—a lot of movement, and it was creating a misunderstanding. The purpose of the misunderstanding was to divide and bring more misunderstanding. Misunderstanding may seem small

---

[20] Go to CourtsOfHeavenWebinars.com to learn about these strategies.

at first, but it can grow within the hearts of men. We were instructed to place a bond upon the people—a Surety Bond.[21]

The Surety Bond

We paused to look up the definition, "A surety bond is a contract between three parties—the principal (you), the **surety** (the Father) and the obligee (the entity requiring the bond)—in which the surety (the Father) guarantees to an obligee that the principal (LifeSpring) will act in accordance with the terms established by the bond.[22] The surety bond provides a guarantee to the obligee (the one receiving ministry) and that the Father will fulfill our obligations (as a ministry) in case of our default.

---

*The bond guarantees
the work gets completed,
that what is promised is performed.*

The work of this ministry, the strength of it, is being felt as a ripple effect. The enemy seeks to divide the ministry. Ezekiel just reminded us of a team members word of knowledge that he had months ago, where he said the Lord had impressed upon him that we, as a

---

[21] Learn about bonds in my book, *Releasing Bonds from the Courts of Heaven*, LifeSpring Publishing (2020).
[22] https://www.suretybonds.com/what-is-a-surety-bond.html

group, needed to continue to release the Bonds of Unity, the Bonds of Health, and Bonds of Safety.

The Courts of Heaven team was experiencing small attacks because a lot of warfare was going on. However, we were assured that Ezekiel, his commanders, and ranks would prevail. We needed to remind our team members, and all that draw near to the ministry, to utilize his commanders and ranks to partner with their angels.

We were reminded of the Scripture that reads, "A thousand shall fall at your side and ten thousand at your right hand. It shall not come near you."[23]

We were then instructed to commission our angels for ordered steps.[24]

> *We commission you to use the veils, the shields, the smoke screens, the curtains, against the enemy, on behalf of all of those that draw near to the ministry and for those who work for LifeSpring and all its components.*

> *We commission you on behalf of this work and those who work with and draw near to LifeSpring, to go with all the angels that are assigned, and to order all our steps from the Lord both in time and out of time, in Jesus' name.*

---

[23] Psalm 91:7
[24] Psalm 37:23

Ezekiel, we commission you to work with each of the angels of those who draw near to his ministry, to instruct them to read their assignees books and scrolls to the people day and night, in Jesus' name.

Father, we ask, in the name of Jesus, to step into Your Court of Titles and Deeds on behalf of all of those who draw near to LifeSpring Ministries, all its employees and their families, Your Honor.

We are requesting a Surety Bond for each one of them, for each member of the Executive Leadership Team, each staff person, and their families, for those that draw near on Tuesday nights, Wednesdays, and those that watch the videos, in the name of Jesus.

We request this be released on behalf of all of those mentioned, to be put upon their records and upon their realms, for Ezekiel, his commanders, and ranks, to bring the surety bonds to each person in the name of Jesus. To place them upon their realms and in their family's realms and upon their household realms. We request this be done both in time and out of time, in Jesus' name

[I want to pause and encourage you to engage your angels and men and women in white in the realms of Heaven for yourself.

If you are having trouble discerning the voice of God, let me encourage you to visit our website, CourtsNet.com and enroll in the online course, *4 Keys to Hearing God's*

Voice. It will aid you in learning how to recognize the voice of the Father when He speaks and learn to capture that information as you learn to journal with Heaven. Don't be satisfied simply to read what we experience. You can experience these things, too.]

Our engagement with Heaven continued and is shared in the next chapter.

———·———

Chapter 5
The Kingdom Dynamic of Trusting Your Steps

The Just Judge continued, "I am also releasing an Assurance Bond, a Bond of Assurance that the people[25] know this work is done. That it is well with your soul."

Stephanie continued,

Thank You, Your Honor, for that. I would also like to Request the Bond of Unity, the Bond of Health, and the Bond of Strength on behalf of the ministry and those that draw near, including their families.

Stephanie noted, "I see paperwork going on. There are a lot of angels standing in line and He is handing this

---

[25] He was speaking of our Courts Of Heaven team and all those who are connected to our ministry (and their families). As you are now reading this, you can request to be included as well.

paperwork to them. Thank You, Your Honor. Thank You for this Court."

Stephanie continued, "I've stepped back into where I had originally seen Ezekiel and he's not here anymore. He's out to do this work.

> *Father, we commend Ezekiel, his commanders, and ranks to You.*
>
> *We commend our own personal angels and all of those that are assigned to us as a ministry to You.*
>
> *We request angel food, bread, and elixir for them as well as every armament of heaven, every Capturing Bag[26] as needed in every color, size, and dimension, in the name of Jesus.*
>
> *We call our angels near and commission them to the full use of these Capture Bags, both in time and out of time and in every dimension, in Jesus' name.*

Stephanie remarked, "Heaven just said, 'No weapon formed against you shall prosper and every tongue that rises against you in judgment you condemn.'" (Isaiah 54:17)

Stephanie replied, "Thank You, Your Honor. Thank you, Heaven."

---

[26] This is discussed in Chapter 9.

Stephanie then realized Lydia was present. She had some instruction for us.

The Kingdom, which Heaven sees as a light in each of us, "So that your light might shine," is a part of us. That *IS* our freedom, and *that* light, we can extend to one another. Let our lights shine. We extend that light to others with our steps upon the earth, in relation to the trust we have with the Father laid out and created as we stood before Him as *Innocence*. Innocence can be defined as our state of being when we originally stood before the Father and accepted our assignment upon the earth. It is also the state of our being that He wants us to live from—the restored state made possible by the resurrection. (See the chapter on the pink capture bags later in this book.)

Innocence is a state of being. Think of the agreement each of us, as Innocence, had with the Father before our steps upon the earth. That original trust *is a* trust we can lean on and glean on. As the has Father *entrusted* IN us, we can trust *IN* Him that our destiny is laid out plainly before us. We can trust that as we agree with Heaven, as we walk, with our light shining—our steps before us that were laid out before the foundation of the earth—we are *trusted* and *entrusted,* **because of our original agreement with the Father.**

---

*We trusted and entrusted,
because of our original agreement
with the Father.*

Stephanie described it this way, "I see Innocence before the Father, where there was an agreement (between Innocence and the Father) and He said this, 'This is your assignment on earth' and then Innocence agreed with it. Then, we (in Innocence) came with our steps upon the earth."

Trusting Your Steps

As long as a person can realize that we have an agreement with the Father, where we stood before Him, that we were *IN* Him *before* time, if we can see the magnitude of that, THAT any trust that has consequential liens upon it where there has been an ungodly trust put on by the enemy, THAT *original trust agreement* between us and the Father, which was laid out in the beginning, is still secure. (The consequential liens can be overcome).

If people can see that, they can trust that every step upon the earth has already been entrusted by the Father to each person.

Trust has been broken. The enemy has put parameters in people's lives where they do not trust the Father. They do not trust themselves. The big picture here is that from the beginning of time, they knew they were loved. They knew they were *entrusted*. They knew that they had an assignment that was bigger than themselves, that *is* mightier than themselves. Our purpose was created before the foundations of the earth. Grasp that. Grasp how deep that is.

Proverbs 8, beginning in verse 22 speaks of this as does Jeremiah 1:5 and several passages in Psalms.

Consider the Lily of the Valley. It, too, has an agreement with the Father. It knew its place upon the earth. It knew when it would grow.[27] It knew how. This is a part of considering who you are in Him.[28]

---

*Many do not understand
or realize they were with Him,
in Him and in front of Him
before they ever took their
first steps upon the earth.*

As people begin to understand, if they can understand it visually or, sense and hear from the Lord and realize that they were in *front* of the Father, that they agreed to come upon this earth with a *very specific mission*, that *THAT* is their value and importance and that *THAT* has not changed. Then their feet can be completely planted in front of them as they walk their destiny out and no matter what sins have been committed along the way (generationally or not), it has not separated their foot in front of them regarding their

---

[27] Ecclesiastes 3:1-8
[28] *"It is through Him that we live and function and have our identity; just as your own poets have said, 'Our lineage comes from Him.'"* (Acts 17:28) (TPT)

mission. It's a surety! That is the surety that they have! The Father is providing the backing that what we say we will deliver, we will deliver because of Him.

The Required Guarantee

This is not limited to one's ministry but includes our individual walk—taking our steps upon the earth. There is still a three-fold cord, as stated in the surety definition, for each of us as an individual. Those around us are the ones requiring the guarantee. The Father is providing the guarantee that what we say, we can deliver on.[29] That is why our light *will* shine! The Father is providing the electricity AND He is guaranteeing it will stay on!

He is also guaranteeing that what we agreed to, at the beginning of time, will be accomplished, if we can grasp the magnitude of that, that we were literally in front of the Father and He was loving on us. Father was speaking into Innocence and Innocence said, "Yes, Father, I will do this."

If each individual person could realize the magnitude of that, they would not be afraid at all. They would not be afraid of walking their steps upon the earth. They would *want* to fulfill their mission. They would also, more importantly, realize they have one. Not only do they have one, but they are equipped for the mission they possess.

---

[29] This is a surety bond that was discussed earlier.

Everything we could ever need for life and complete devotion to God has already been deposited in us by His divine power. *For all this was lavished upon us through the rich experience of knowing Him who has called us by name and invited us to come to Him through a glorious manifestation of His goodness. (2 Peter 1:3 TPT) (Emphasis added)*

We are not tossed aside because of a sin!

If we have a flat tire, we fix the tire. Recently, the Father said concerning us, that He was personally backing with a personal guarantee and the paperwork said it was a "Personal Guarantee"—just like He co-signed a loan.

This is Kingdom Dynamics. Malcolm had told us we had much more to learn about Kingdom Dynamics. He was right!

Walking on Water

In finalizing this book, Stephanie and I checked in with Heaven for any final instructions regarding the content of the book and we were impressed to add two more recent revelations to the overall book. What follows is the revelation we received as we engaged with Peter, the apostle.

This day we had our first engagement with Peter. As he walked up to us, he affirmed that he was the Peter from the New Testament and he said, "I walked in the 'strength' and in 'adjudication." To adjudicate is to act as a judge in a court case and render a decision in the case. By strength, he was implying that he learned to walk in the strength of the Courts of Heaven, rather than his own strength. We had a couple of examples from Peter's life where that did not work out too well for him.

Peter said, "Remind the people that in their weakness, HE is strong, especially in the court processes. This is where you lean not upon your own understanding. The people will bear much fruit in their court work when they work in that humility."

Peter then handed Stephanie a scroll that had the words, "Next Steps" written on it. He said that he would be coming alongside of us. It felt like he was joining our team. I took the scroll and placed it in my heart.

Peter continued, "You want to talk about governing? I had to learn it the hard way. I'm here *to bring ease* in the matter. Governing is not just a tool, it's a right. It's truly where there is *strength and adjudication*. The perception has been that a person is too weak in their understanding to go into the courts. It is not in their strength. If they could go into the courts with the mindset of where they are weak, He is strong, then there will be strength in the adjudication process for every person. It is truth. This is not in and of yourself. Lean on counsel, lean on Wisdom."

Stephanie asked, "Peter, how did you struggle with this?"

Peter replied, "I had walked with Jesus. I thought I knew everything. It was only the beginning. Today, I am here for such a time as this because revelation will soon be coming to you at lightning speed."

Stephanie remarked, "Thank you, Peter, that you're going to be bringing ease for this to everyone. I find it interesting that you're telling us you're going to be bringing us lightning speed revelation."

Peter added, "The Father never gives you more than you can handle."

Stephanie replied, "So what you're saying is, *we can handle lightning speed revelation.* Amen. Hallelujah! That's all glory to God."

I asked, "Can we take a look at the next steps scroll now?"

Peter responded, "I thought you would never ask."

Stephanie noticed that suddenly Peter was walking on water. We remembered that Peter was the one that got out of the boat, and he had always been razzed for sinking in the water while everybody else was safely in the boat.

Peter said, "What if I told you, you could do this, too?"

Stephanie replied, "Well, many of us have read your story, Peter, and all of us have said, "Well, if Jesus said we would do these things and greater, we believed it in our head but not necessarily in our hearts."

Peter added, "Why do you think I sunk? I got all up in my head. Walking on water, it isn't head knowledge. It never can be. Everything is a spiritual matter." (When he said 'matter,' he just showed us the matter that the water is made of.)

He asked, "What's the matter with this matter? (Now he raised his feet up showing us the matter of what our bodies are made of.) What is the matter with that matter? It's heavy and it sinks, doesn't it? But,

---

If you were spirit forward, your spirit would carry your body."

Stephanie exclaimed, "Wow, WOW, Wow! I'm blown away right now! *Our spirit will carry our body!*

"You blew my mind for a second because I saw our spirit come forward and be like the bubble with our body inside of it."

I added, "And bubbles can float."

Peter explained, "When Jesus called me onto the water, my spirit man *was* forward. I was excited realizing that was Jesus out on the water—the one that I loved, my brother, the one I believed in so much. Before I realized what I was even doing, I was on the water. Then I got into my head and my spirit man took a back seat and my soul came forward. That is why I began to sink. Don't get me wrong, I believed the principle of being spirit forward. It will make you think every time, in every situation."

> *Live spirit forward
> and you will walk on water.*

With that closing comment, Peter was gone.

Stephanie remarked, "Look at the revelation you were given about living spirit forward, and now we're going to come to this new thing of *being* spirit forward and *knowing* we can walk on water. This is also where we are going to be able to suddenly be in a different place! I love Heaven. Wow!"

40

Chapter 6
The Kingdom Dynamics of Trusts

Stephanie and I had accessed the Business Complex of Heaven specifically to learn about the concept of trusts. Although we had some natural understanding of the legal agreements known as trusts of various types, we had little understanding of heavenly trusts.

We took a seat in the classroom where we had been taken and Malcolm, the man in white who often advises and teaches us in our ministry, was present to teach us.

There are bondages that *look* like trusts, that *sound* like trusts, that even *feel* like trusts in the natural. These bondages prevent explorations in Heaven, Kingdom Dynamics of Heaven, Throne Room entries of Heaven, and even the simplicities of income. These are bondages. It is a parameter that the enemy has put around someone's access into the aforementioned places.

Heaven has placed Godly trusts on each of our lives. They are legal agreements granting access to certain benefits, provisions, or designs of Heaven. The enemy, who is a copy-cat, seeks to pervert these Godly trusts by placing allegations or parameters against them, basically to invalidate them. These creations are essentially ungodly trusts.

A definition of an ungodly trust is this:

An ungodly trust is a legal document from the enemy. See it as an indictment. The parameters and what is inside of them are the iniquity/ iniquities carried through the generations. Think of it like this, the ungodly trust is the legal document, and the parameters are what is written on that document (the crimes committed/the allegations) that the prosecution is using against a person. Because it is a legal document originating from the courts of hell, it can be cancelled from the Courts of Heaven, specifically in the Court of Cancellations.

It can be seen in other times, in other realms, and other dimensions—in time and out of time. That is how it is structured in the kingdom of darkness.

Part of the dynamics of the Kingdom of Heaven is to get these ungodly trusts removed from our lives so that we function in all the fullness the Father planned for us before we were. The enemy takes what would be the goods of Heaven, the access, the entrances, the gifts, the knowledge, and even portals, and hijacks them using evil timelines, using the spirit of fear in people's lives, using spiritual droughts because of the spirit of religion in people's lives, and using bitterness and unforgiveness. This is how Godly trusts are taken into a form of captivity due to the parameters placed on the Godly trust (for example) on why someone is unable to access the things that are the Kingdom of Heaven.

In essence, the enemy hijacks a Godly trust and by placing parameters (which are allegations) on that trust, he places a particular type of lien (known as a consequential lien) upon that trust. He stops or hinders the benefits of that Godly trust from ever impacting the life of the believer. Typically, the parameters are allegations or indictments against a person that usually come from iniquity in that person's bloodline. These consequential liens typically have a principality behind it due to the iniquity in the bloodline. Once the iniquity is repented of on behalf of the generational line, one can request their angels to strike (or remove) the parameters that were placed against the Godly trust. Once stricken the person then has free access to the benefits of the Godly trust.

The setting of these parameters against the Godly trusts are strategies of Hell, not unlike what we can read about in Aprile Osborne's book[30] of the meetings of the counsels of hell and what occurs in those gatherings.

---

[30] *Seeing Behind Enemy Lines* by Aprile Osborne. Destiny Image (2019).

When we discern an ungodly strategy against someone or against a business/ministry/family, etc., we simply repent for the iniquity in the bloodline, request the cancellation of that ungodly strategy that arose from the counsels of hell (we request this in the Court of Cancellations). The ungodly strategy did not have the backing of Heaven and as we are a son of God, once the repentance is complete, the ungodly strategy has no legal right to continue. It is a trespass of the enemy.

Remember, any legal paperwork from the courts/counsels of Hell can be overturned in the superior court system of the Courts of Heaven.

Unfortunately, the church has been taught for generations that if evil things happen to us, it must have been the will of God for that to occur. We have gotten our theology from a song sung by Doris Day in the Alfred Hitchcock film, "The Man Who Knew Too Much" (1956). The lyrics were, "*Que sera sera*, whatever will be will be. The future's not ours to see, *que sera sera*."

Those are hardly scriptural lyrics and form a poor basis of Christian theology, but that is essentially the approach taken by many believers and by many modern churches. We may have held to a similar belief system once upon a time. If so, we want to repent of that. Just because something happens, that does not mean that was the design of Heaven for our life.

> *Walk in our sonship which includes the authority that a son of God possesses.*

The Kingdom of Heaven can easily gain back this access to the things belonging to the sons on behalf of the sons. Some will be through fasting, but most will be through the paradigms of prayer and courtroom work. This is like what we already know about the dynamics of the Court of Cancellations and the cancellation of these parameters/allegations done through repentance work for coming into agreement with the spirit of fear, for embracing doubt, for embracing the spirit of religion, all of which we have been taught to break. This work will be done through the Court of Cancellations.

How will we identify a parameter on Godly trust?

When clients/people are unable to obtain breakthrough in their everyday lives of freedoms that they know are available to them, the removal of the parameters from Godly trusts provides one more point of access through the Courts of Heaven for freedom. This is easily handled in the Court of Cancellations because of Jesus and because of His love for the people. This is part of the provision. This is part of the finished work of Jesus.

> Will it show up in the registry as well if we are looking for it?

If we are looking for it, we can see it. Our advocates have been instructed to look for Consequential Liens and to look for the ungodly parameters on a trust. There is a simplicity of how we do work in the courts anyway. Envision someone going to the Mercy Court, where there had been unforgiveness, or doubt, or partnering with the spirit of religion. Then going to the Court of Cancellations and severing the spirit of religion and giving the title deeds back to Jesus.

The Senior Advocates have access to that prayer paradigm. When they see this come up, this is a prayer that they can have the person in front of them pray against the spirit of religion that will break off the parameters.[31] There are some that come that need that specifically done. This will open a floodgate where there are no longer conditions or limitations to their freedoms, and their access, their gifts, their incomes. This is not an extra *layer* of freedom; it is an extra *tool* for freedom.

---

[31] See the blog post, "Divorcing the Spirit of Religion" https://www.courtsofheavenwebinars.com/post/court-case-divorcing-the-spirit-of-religion

Prayer for Freedom from Religion

Father, in the name of Jesus, I request access to the Court of Cancellations.

I repent for partnering with religion instead of partnering with You.

I repent for giving religion and the spirit of religion lordship over my life.

I repent where I surrendered the title deed of my faith over to the spirit of religion.

I repent for those in my ancestry who did the same. I ask Your forgiveness, in the name of Jesus.

I forgive those in my ancestral line who did the same.

I ask that every parameter against my life and my generations be stricken from the Godly trusts You have for my life.

I call my angels near and commission them to strike every parameter affected by my repentance.

I choose to surrender the title deed of this area of my life over to You, in the name of Jesus.

Thank You for freedom, Your Honor.

Are there different kinds of trusts?

In the natural, we have different kinds of trusts. Malcolm illustrated by drawing a giant parenthesis on a whiteboard. We heard the word 'parameter.'[32] All the allegations against the saint are written inside of those parentheses. It is *all encompassing*. That is the simplicity of Heaven.

We already know that some find the Courtrooms of Heaven daunting. This is not daunting work. Heaven is not making it more complicated. We just didn't know anything about it. This is just part of the tools in the tool set. There will be more coming down the pike.

---

*All parameters of trusts
will be dealt with in
the Court of Cancellations.*

A Consequential Lien is easily satisfied by the blood of Jesus. Often, there is repentance for the action that opened the door to the allegation in the bloodline that is needed, but if it was illegally done, no repentance is necessary. We can simply request the striking of the parameters if it was illegally done.[33]

---

[32] A parameter is essentially an allegation.
[33] In this case, no repentance was required as I had done nothing to precipitate this consequential lien. It was an act of trespass by the enemy.

Father, I'm requesting that the lien placed upon me via the parameter placed against this trust by the enemy against the open doors that the Kingdom of Heaven has for me, I request it be completely removed from me.

We may see the parameter with the word 'lien' in the middle of it being washed with living water mixed with the blood of Jesus. The lien is collapsing under the movement of the water and the blood. In that instance, the movement is like a frequency because movement *is* as a frequency.

We were instructed to teach the advocates[34] **to commission the angels to go and remove the evil parameters because we all have ungodly trusts[35] that Heaven wants removed.** The enemy is the one that puts the parameters in place, creating the ungodly trust.

Commission the angels to remove the parameters that the enemy has placed on the trust.

---

[34] Referring to our Senior and Junior Advocates who lead our Personal Advocacy Sessions.

[35] When parameters are placed against a Godly trust, it essentially creates an ungodly trust. By the removal of the parameters, the trust is cleared, and we can experience the benefits of that now Godly trust.

"Then, commission them to strike the parameters,"[36] Malcolm directed us.

"In this instance, they are to strike the parameters—the indictments. The act of striking invalidates them or removes them from the trust."

Heaven has trusts on us, but the enemy comes to interfere with us and our trusts. When we are born, trusts are one of the things that the enemy can see. These trusts are part of the Kingdom Dynamics we live from, and they are very specifically upon us and upon our DNA. The trust that Heaven has given us has multiple meanings to it.

The trust provides open access to the Father and all the Kingdom Dynamics that were mentioned before.

The enemy comes in to put parameters (indictments) on that trust to keep us from walking in the fullness of the Father's Kingdom.

Commission your angels to strike the parameters.

---

[36] To "strike the parameters" is akin to the legal jargon of "striking from the record" which means to remove it as if it had never been in the record.

In the name of Jesus, I call Ezekiel, his commanders, and his ranks to come near. I call Stephanie's angels near.

We commission you to strike the parameters the enemy has placed on the trusts that the Lord has granted to us so that we can fulfill the purpose and destiny of God in fullness and all the Kingdom Dynamics that the Father wants us to walk in.

Proverbs 3:5-6 reads:

Trust in the LORD with all your heart, and lean not on your own understanding and in all your ways acknowledge Him and He will direct your paths.

There is a play on words where we read: 'Trust in the Lord,' but the Father is making it a legal document.

Notice the wording of
'trust in the Lord with all your heart.'
It is **a permission slip** to trust
the Lord with all your heart.

We already have that as part of our DNA to be able to trust in the Lord with *ALL* our heart. Religion has tried to stop that right to trust the Lord in that manner. Fear has tried to stifle it. All the junk that has happened in our life is just to keep us from trusting with *all* our heart, but that's the trust. If there is any lien (or any parameters are placed) against that trust, we can get that canceled in the

Court of Cancellations. We can look and see what other things that are 'Trusts' *of* the Lord, like there are other verses that say, 'trust in the Lord.' Look in Psalms (and Proverbs) and we will find other things that are types of trusts.

These are how we are to teach people to look in the same in similar order to how we see the Bond Registry's Personal Page, et cetera. This is how we are to view this. People can go in and look at this Trust Registry. People want a simplistic understanding of what the next step is. This is step by step.

I have seen several names and the first is:

- **Trust of Trust** – where people trust us. The original design of the Father was that we live life without suspicion. We were designed for trust, but the enemy has interfered. *Trust of Trust is the trust fund the Father has created for us and all that encompasses.*

The one below that is:

- **Trust of the Father** – not as your daughters see you, but as people see *you* as a father figure.

Below the trust as a father is:

- **Trust as a son/daughter** – that's us and our relationship with the Father.

Next there is:

- **Trust as Income** – under that are categories of:

- **Trust of Work** – the Father has created us with unique abilities and skill sets that are designed to be rewarded by others. We have a particular ability to do a certain thing, we find that thing and are employed for it. As a result, we sow time and effort, and the reward is financial provision. The better we are at what we do, the more we are rewarded. We are told that if we want to eat, we must work.[37]

The next is:

- **Trust of Stewardship** – which includes tithes, offerings, first fruits, etc.

   We must evaluate where we stand regarding this aspect of trust. We have been taught (mostly by religion) *not* to trust the Father as provider. We have been taught that the Father cannot be depended upon. This is a lie. *The fact that we have experienced provision in the past, prophesies that we will have provision in the future.*

   Do we trust His provision for us? Do we trust him that we will survive if we dedicate 10% of our income to Him as a tithe? **The tithe is a barometer of trust in**

---

[37] 2 Thessalonians 3:10

the arena of finances. Offerings is the next level of trust in that arena, followed by first fruits, and alms. All are levels of trust that we develop with the Father, the provider of all.

The next one is the:

- **Trust as a Friend** – under that is:

    - **Trust of a friend that sticks closer than a brother** – to be that to someone on that level requires a level of trust and a willingness to live in forgiveness.

    Then:

    - **Trust of a friend to all** – I see that as just the Kingdom Dynamics of being good to everybody, being a nice guy or nice lady.

    We typically don't see relationships as issues of trust, but really, they are *all about* trust. We cannot have a relationship without trust. The moment we stop trusting the other party, the relationship suffers. How are we doing in that arena?

Under that is the:

- **Trust of Ministry** – you are reading this book or listening to this teaching based on a level of trust that I will have something to say that benefits you and does not harm you. I hope to live up to that trust. We all have been harmed by those in leadership in the church. Some did the harm maliciously, but most probably did not. You have experienced deep wounds. I, too, have been wounded.

The Trust of Ministry arena has multiple sides to it. The subcategories Malcolm pointed out are:

- **Trust of Platform** – do we trust the person on the platform? When the person on the platform violates that trust, will we forgive them as we have been forgiven, or will we allow that situation to taint our view of others in the ministry? Will we allow it to bleed over in not trusting God, who called that person to ministry?

- **Trust of Prayer** – wrapped up in the Trust of Ministry is the question we must ask ourselves. Do we trust prayer? Many have been disappointed when they did not see the desired result of something they may have prayed for over a long period of time. Some have found relief and a new measure of hope in the Courts of Heaven paradigm, but it is not an answer in all things. It is a set of tools that we can utilize to invite Heaven into our situations. Still, some have been disappointed in this paradigm as well. We must remember, prayer is not a vending machine where I put a certain phrase or phrases into the slot and out comes the answer. Prayer is the invitation to Heaven into our situation.

- **Trust of Seed** – immediately when I saw 'seed,' it took me directly to the teaching we heard from Amanda Winder[38] and the word 'seed' was in gold. We implement those kinds of things in the slot of that trust. We look if there are liens, issues, or problems that need to be canceled. We can do these things in a prayer paradigm.

However, one of the implications of the Trust of Seed reflects to the Parable of the Sower in Mark 4. Jesus pointed out that in that parable, the seed was the Word of God. The question is, "How are we doing in our trust of the Word of God?"

Many of us aren't doing too well in that category. We read our Bible, but it isn't alive to us. It is stories on a page. If it is stories on a page, then something needs to be fixed in the trust arena. We had just been taught what that means from Amanda.

---

[38] See the blog post by Amanda Winder at https://amandawinder.com/2022/01/20/multiplication-part-ii/ Amanda is a former Team Member.

- **Trust of Kings** – this involved the ability to trust the office a person stands in spiritually and otherwise.

The list continued:

- **Trust of Family** – there are three categories:

  - **Trust of Biological Family** – do we trust our mom and dad or our siblings? Our grandparents and cousins? Uncles and aunts? Many have had biological family that violated trust with us, and this is a difficult area to reconcile, but Heaven needs us to look again and will help us to forgive the violators and find healing and restoration. We must forgive as we have been forgiven. Paul instructed us in Ephesians 4:32: *And be kind to one another, tenderhearted, forgiving one another, even as God in Christ forgave you.*

    Heaven wants all parties to be living out of their original design, not out of their brokenness.

The second category of family is:

  - **Trust of Close Friends** – those that are close like a brother. It goes up to that one under Trust as a Friend that says, 'a friend that sticks closer than a brother.'

The other one under family is the:

- **Trust of the Family of God** – this is our literal brothers and sisters in Christ. Are we walking in love with them? Are we willing to offer a degree of trust to them, and even if they mess up, forgive them? These are hard questions sometimes, because wounds from a friend, from a brother or sister in the faith, are often tough pills to swallow. If we have experienced traumatic things because of trusting a brother or sister in Christ, are we willing to trust again?

The division created by violations of trust are simply to make an example of us to the world. Will we take the bait?

Other categories and subcategories may exist, but these are what we were shown at the time. This is basically a Trust Registry and what we have been describing is our Personal page on our Trust Registry. But realize that because this is our Personal page, this Personal page affects all the other pages.

Every parameter is an allegation against some form of trust. Most often the enemy will place parameters against our Trust of the Father, or Trust as a Son. Once the parameters are removed through repentance, freedom to trust in these areas will come to us.

Whenever we see a parameter, ask Heaven to show what arena of trust that parameter is against. Another way to see this is to request to view the person's Trust Registry. Then look for any trusts that are noted that have allegations that are against that arena of trust.

Then begin the repentance for where that entered the bloodline and where it was perpetuated in the bloodline. Ask the angels to strike the parameters/allegations and remove them from the person's life. We will see it stricken through or removed from the person's registry as we do this. Request access to the Court of Trade and ask for the eviction of the principality from off that arena of trust.

Personal Trust Registries

As we were receiving this revelation, we realized that Heaven had a Trust Registry for each person. Appearing somewhat like the Bond Registry, this list contained the various types of trusts that involve people and shows which type has been impacted by a consequential lien.[39] The Trust Registry shows us areas of trust in our lives that need strengthening or rebuilding. The information about whether we are dealing with a consequential lien or parameters against a Godly trust can be accessed multiple ways. One can search in a person's Guest Registry which contains information about intruders;

---

[39] If you identify a consequential lien, know that you have parameters against some area of trust in that person's life.

lingering human spirits; spirit, soul, or body fragmentation; and much more.

Now we understood that we could discover what areas of trust in a person's life had been affected by a consequential lien, or ungodly trust.[40] Another way to see about a consequential lien is to request to investigate the Outstanding Folder. Heaven simply wants us to have the information and has made a myriad of ways available to us to discover what we need to experience freedom.

Once repentance was accomplished for the sin that opened the door for a principality to create a consequential lien and any parameters had been stricken, the area of trust that had been impacted would be marked "Cleared" in the Trust Registry. If a particular area of trust was still impacted, it would be highlighted or noted in the Trust Registry.

When looking in the Bond Registry and seeing a consequential lien in place, ask the question, "Which trust is this against?"

Remember, the whole point of a consequential lien is to keep us from access

---

[40] The enemy at times will place an ungodly trust against someone. Follow the same procedure for removing parameters to gain freedom.

> *to our inheritance of the trust
> the Father has established for us.*

When we see a parameter attached to a consequential lien or to a trust, we automatically know it is against one of those areas of trust.

As people are coming to know me and this ministry related to false accusations and parameters, the enemy would try to take those accusations and put parameters around this legislative office under the Trust of Trust. The enemy would try to put parameters so there would be loss of trust towards me, the ministry personally, the Courts of Heaven, about CourtsNet, and about Sandhills Ecclesia.

> *The aim of the enemy in this
> is so a hardness of heart develops
> in us so we don't trust other people.*

We realized this is a revelation, not unlike the bond revelation. It can be used the way we review a bond registry. It has the same usefulness, and it has the same ability to disclose parameters/allegations.

As part of the message, many have lost trust and faith in Father God, because of the different trusts that have parameters inside of them from the enemy, as these parameters are eliminated, the trust between their heavenly Father and themselves will be reignited. People will be able to understand the depth of it, through the format we are releasing.

---

*Trusting the Father
is something many struggle with.*

---

*The striking of the parameters
will reignite the levels of love and
heavenly downloads from the Father.*

———·———

Chapter 7
The Kingdom Dynamics of Accessed Inheritance

Why it is we have trouble understanding things about the Word, things about Holy Spirit, things about walking in truth and knowledge? Why have we not been able to walk in all the power and understanding?

We must glean the principle and understanding of the son now. Many that are ripe for this understanding—many that will choose to glean and begin walking as a son, will begin partaking of their place of authority. Some are just beginning to step into Heaven.

> *Heaven wants them to know that this gleaning is a trade.*

Just the acceptance of this gleaning, the acceptance of the indwelling of the Holy Spirit, and acceptance of all that the Kingdom of Heaven has for us His sons, each of these are in fact a trade. In fact, this is the Trust of Trust. The trust that is inheritance which was laid before the foundations of the world. The trust that we as sons can indeed trust our Father, that we have this access to the full inheritance of Heaven. No more disassociation.

Our Father has indeed presented to His sons the trust of this inheritance, with the parameters being the blood and faith. The realities are that we can fully access every inheritance—the inheritance that is freedom, the inheritance that is love, the inheritance that is mercies of Heaven, the inheritance that is the Glory, the inheritance that is health, the inheritance that is victory.

This is a reality, not merely a reality in the spiritual—this is a reality in the natural.

How do we get that from the spiritual into the natural?

For the concept of understanding how a trust is built in the natural we will need to understand:

There is an actual trust that has been built in the Kingdom of Heaven for the sons.

We do not have to die to get this. It is here for us now! We can access this trust now! We do not have to be of a certain age or have an attorney present, because we have counsel in Heaven. We do not have to have these other parameters. The only parameter is the blood of Jesus Christ—with accepting Him as our savior and faith. That is the only parameter. That alone has given us this trust that we have access to and that when we have freedom from these consequential liens that the enemy has put upon us, we are free from those princes. We truly have this full freedom and access to the Kingdom of Heaven.

How do we apply this? How does this work where it is truly seen in the natural?

Heaven is trying to help us really be free in our hearts and our minds. This is a part of standing in the sun. Envision a ship on tumultuous water and the hand of God picks the ship up and takes it out of the water. That is how we are as sons with this inheritance.

Do we trust? The Father earnestly wants us to rightfully take our places as sons to experience it. Not just to know it in our minds, but to experience it, to walk in it, to be seated in it, to stand in the authority of it, ruling from Heaven down, seated as sons in heavenly places with Jesus. This is the next level.

Some of us are like the many people sitting in churches and hearing that they are seated as sons in heavenly places and are not comprehending it at all. They have no concept of it. Some are believing it, but not knowing how to walk in it—not knowing how to fulfill that in their own lives.

For them, the need is to understand this Kingdom Dynamic, that this is their inheritance. It is a major part of their inheritance, **that they can be seated in heavenly places with Jesus Christ ruling and reigning and walking this out with Jesus.** That is where the freedom, the healing, the understanding, wisdom, and knowledge and walking in that in their natural lives will play out. That is the promise.

Romans 8:19-21:

"For the earnest expectation of the creature waited for the manifestation of the sons of God. [20] For against its will, the universe itself has had to endure the empty futility resulting from the consequences of human sin. But now, with eager expectation, [21] all creation longs for freedom from its slavery to decay and to experience with us the wonderful freedom coming to God's children.

Now compare:

"Our lives now represent the one event. Every creature anticipates with held breath, standing on tiptoe, as it were, to witness the unveiling of the sons of God. Can you hear the drum roll? [20] every creature suffered abuse through Adam's fall. They were discarded like a squeezed-out Orange, creation did not volunteer to fall prey to the effect of the fall. Yet within the stark setting, hope prevails. All creation knows that the glorious liberty of the sons of God sets the stage

for their own release from decay." (THE MIRROR)

In verse 21, the Mirror commentary says, "I am concerned for you that you might pine away through the illusion of separation from Christ and that just like Eve, you might become blurry-eyed and deceived into believing a lie about yourselves. The temptation was to exchange the truth about our completeness [I am] with the idea of incompleteness [I am not], and shame; thinking that perfection required your toil in all manner of weariness labor!"

Many that are following us that hear this and they know it in their mind, but they do not understand who they are as sons. That must be revealed from Heaven, just like Peter, when asked by Jesus, "Who do you say that I am?" Peter answered from the revelation of Heaven who Jesus was. Ask Heaven to make it real to you.

In Numbers 27 we were taught that an inheritance can be distributed, but we must possess it for it to impact us. (This is discussed more in chapter 10.)

As we walk our journey, we can look down and see that our steps are right beside those Heaven has sent to assist us. That is part of our inheritance. As we walk in the natural, as we are stepping into our inheritance, fully embracing and understanding what that means—with the trust of trust in the process, we can look down and see that our steps are in sync and right next to Heaven's. We are tangibly at their side.

As we walk in the natural, look up and see that Jesus is facing us and we are facing him. That is an inheritance. Not only is Jesus beside us, He is also behind us, guarding us from the rear.

There is not a place that we step upon the earth that His step is not coordinated with ours. This is our inheritance.

That is our inheritance.

Choosing our inheritance is key.

We must lay down old mindsets and accept the keys to freedom. There are many keys that Heaven wants to extend to the people regarding their inheritance, but it is a choice. Choose the inheritance to see Jesus' steps next to ours, to look up and see His face before us, to know that His steps are coordinated with ours—even behind us. Choose *that* inheritance. Choose the inheritance that is the trust of the Kingdom—that has been given to us as a son. It is a glorious day when there are those that are choosing their inheritance.

Seeing Jesus' feet next to ours is incredibly impactful. As we walk in our normal life, we can have the comfort of knowing that as we are walking, we can look down and know that Jesus' feet are next to ours, in front of ours, behind ours, and beside ours.

> *Sometimes it is the simplest things that people need to grasp and hear to create profound accelerations in their life.*

What we learned was about the trust of trust, because the trust of trust is the trust fund that God has created in Heaven for us—all that means, all it encompasses, and how we can walk in it. When Adam and Eve were in the garden before the fall, they walked in the full access of their inheritance.

The Consequential Lien

When we see a consequential lien, the first question we need to ask is, "Which trust is this against?"

The whole point of the consequential lien is to prevent you from full access into your inheritance—your inheritance as a son, your inheritance as a minister or the platform you use. You have your inheritance to the full Kingdom of Heaven—all of that.

> *The whole point of the consequential lien is to keep you from access to your inheritance of the trust that the Father has established for you.*

All that Heaven has for us, we have access to as a son. Do we *trust* the Father? Are *we* trustworthy? We have the full *trust of Heaven*, which is our inheritance. Is there a lien on just that ability to trust? Is there a lien on our health? Is there a lien on our ability to trust as a friend?

When we see a parameter, we automatically know it is against one of those trusts.

The whole point of a consequential lien is that a prince has been assigned to keep you from being able to access your inheritance, to keep you boxed in.

He also uses our generational iniquities in our bloodline against us to keep us boxed in and keep us from accessing all our inheritance.

The Trust of Trust is the trust fund that the Father has created for us and all that encompasses.

How would we best describe the trust registry columns that are in it?

Heaven is prepared for us. Not only is it for us at the end of our life, but it is also here. It is for the *here* and *now*—this place of interaction, but there has been a trust issue. The Father longs for this place for us now.

> *The joy of walking in the
> here and now of this trust
> opens all the keys.*

We **have** an inheritance right now! We **have access** to our inheritance right now! We **can access** our inheritance **right now!**

Heaven has prepared a place before us in Heaven with keys at every seat at the table. The chairs may be empty right now, but the Father is saying we can come sit at the table and partake of these Kingdom principles. "The Lord has prepared a table in the presence of their enemies."[41] When we are seated at this table, our enemies may appear, but they are not so big anymore. They are not seated at the table, either. They are not even invited to the table. *We* are seated at the table that is *in the presence* of our enemies. THAT is good news!

---

[41] Psalm 23:5

Chapter 8
The Kingdom Dynamics of Transition

Kingdom dynamics, is fun, isn't it? We had a question concerning the transition into Heaven of human spirits. We asked, "When a person passes away and they become a spirit that stays behind as a lingering human spirit, those that had a principality, do they have an ungodly trust that kept them from entering Heaven?"

Picture someone at their death bed, and as soon as they slip away or are coming out of their body, they see what we call the portal in front of them that lets them transition to eternity. They see angels, but sometimes demons can be seen. The reality is, when a person passes away, they have full knowledge of all spiritual entities. The veil has been removed. In the moment of their passing, they are given the choice to transition into eternity or to pause, but do you really think the enemy stops his lies at the point of death?

> *What is done from Satan's kingdom,*
> *it is not just to hurt the sons,*
> *it is to hurt the Father.*

Satan hates the Father! The enemy knows there is restoration in the work of helping lingering human spirits transition to Heaven. His goal is to keep them from the Kingdom of Heaven as long as possible.

Impediments to Transition

The picture was of a person standing after death in what we would think of as outer space. It's the space between us (while alive) and the other side of the veil. You can see angels and demons, as well as the person that died. As that person steps out of their body, if they have had a consequential lien or an ungodly parameter put upon their trust, which is their inheritance, see this prince standing there saying to them, "You have no access. Look at what all you and your generations have done!" He is scaring them into believing that they don't have access to their inheritance and that IF they *do* go in through the portal (the silver channel) to Heaven that there is only judgment awaiting them![42] Satan is just using us and LHS's to hurt the Father over and over and

---

[42] See my book, *Lingering Human Spirits*, LifeSpring Publishing (2020).

over. We have that old preaching that says you must be judged when you die.

We can envision it as if we are the one that is standing there, and we see what is considered light and what is considered darkness on the other side of the veil. Can we imagine stepping out of our body and there's a principality standing there saying, "Oh no, you don't have a way in there!" Then you have an angel saying, "Come on, it's time, come on with me." Then the prince says, "Oh no! You've been way too bad. You're going to be judged."

When they were living, consider if ungodly parameters were placed upon their trust, which is the absolute walking in and stepping into your inheritance when you are alive, but and when they die, they face that scenario. When we say the verse, "I am the way the truth and the life,"[43] the Father has literally provided this way for those who believed in life after death, that felt they didn't deserve to step into Heaven, or were still in bondage and couldn't step over. Jesus is saying, "No, *I* am the way."

The enemy even knew that there is a way and that the people of light—us, were going come into this concept and understanding of LHS work, provide help, co-laboring with Heaven, and open the portal for them to go through! That's why Satan didn't want the church to know about this revelation—ever!

---

[43] John 14:6

People are going to die that aren't going to make the choice to come on into Heaven because they still are living under that demon or that prince that is lying to them at the point of their death, but God is saying "I'm still providing a way, and I'm doing it through my sons that are living."

The fact that the enemy will do all he can to hinder us accessing Heaven either now, or ultimately, needs to be understood. Dealing with the ungodly parameters against our lives and lineage needs to be dealt with. It can have eternal consequences.

Part of the Kingdom Dynamics of Heaven is to live free from every bondage.

We just have not thought about this arena as being an area of bondage for many, but we can help them out.

Chapter 9
The Kingdom Dynamics
of Capture Bags

The next several chapters are included in this book because they have relevance when ministering to lingering human spirits. They are from my book, Lingering Human Spirits – Volume 2. *They deal with a tool/weapon known as Capture Bags that angels use in behalf of us as sons and on behalf of the Kingdom.*

Stephanie and I had engaged Heaven, and Ezekiel appeared carrying a red bag. Knowing that things like colors are not accidental in Heaven, we asked about it. We were told it was a capturing bag and that he had captured an infiltration. He did not expound on that.

He wanted to teach us about capture bags, so we welcomed his instruction. The capturing bags are very important to be released and commissioned to the angels. The size of them matters. Begin to see, as you release capturing bags, the various sizes. There will be different sizes for different means. The one Ezekiel was carrying was a large size because he dealt with a large infiltration, and it was necessary and needed for this specific capture. There are other capturing bags that will be of different colors. Each one of the various colors represents not only a color, but a size, depending upon the capture needed. Equip the angels with all the sizes. They are representative of a specific task, and it is what they use for specific captures.

The red bag, representing having the blood of Jesus infused in it, was needed and necessary to keep the capture of the infiltration Ezekiel was carrying.

Once they have captured the infiltration, they will destroy it along with the bag. There is a never-ending supply of the different sizes that represent the colors of the bags. Within the bag one could see what appeared to be a grid keeping the infiltration in the bag.

Ezekiel explained that it was part of the dismantling that is taking place on the earth today. These capturing bags are not new to angels, but they are new to us, especially regarding the different sizes and their meanings. He pointed out that this will be an important part that the ecclesia/the people will need to understand while commissioning their angels. It's a tool.

This will be an important part that the ecclesia/the people will need to understand while commissioning their angels. They are considered classifications in Heaven. There are some that are classifications for small demons—things that are easily captured or easily contained. Then there are some that are classified specifically for domains. It will capture a whole domain. This is where the fun begins when capturing domains.

An aspect of the authority that you have through Jesus to commission angels, is the capturing of these domains—the collapsing of these domains. Other angels will be around with other classifications of these capturing bags, capturing the entities trying to flee. This is a part of a strategy of Heaven given to the saints to walk in freedom—to walk in their freedom and victory.

At this stage of learning, we were told to commission the angels with the classifications. Request all the classifications of the capture bags. We would soon learn about the different classifications that are represented as colors. He explained that the red one is one of the larger ones and it was not the one for domains, but it was used for infiltrations.

Capture Bag Commission

Ezekiel reminded us that the enemy would continue to try to infiltrate. That is why the classification of these bags is so important and the commissioning of the angels is so important. The people's commissioning of their angels with these is so important. It will prevent the infiltration into their own lives.

Worm holes are a type of infiltration. The capturing bags are things angels use as a tool—as a part of the dismantling of those infiltrations.

Angelic Commissioning

[Feel free to modify this commissioning for your angels and your situation.]

I call Ezekiel, his commanders, and his ranks, along with my angels to come near.

Father, I request on behalf of the angels, all the different sizes, classifications, and colors of every capturing bag needed to serve the Kingdom of Heaven and to serve Your people, in Jesus' name.

Ezekiel, I commission you, your commanders, and your ranks to use the classifications of every capturing bag needed; to go and capture the infiltrations; to use the different colors and classifications of the bags as needed from the smallest demon to the largest domain, in the name of Jesus; to use these capturing bags throughout our realms and over LifeSpring, Sandhills Ecclesia, CourtsNet, and the other facets of LifeSpring, along with those that are at work on behalf of these ministries and for their families, in Jesus' mighty name.

He instructed us to include their families because this was a type of covering.

Immediately, we saw Ezekiel with his arms loaded with various colors and sizes of capture bags. Within seconds, he left to make use of the bags. With that,

Ezekiel was finished with this brief training on capture bags.

Black Capture Bags

Stephanie and I were in a classroom engaging with Ezekiel, when he began to teach on black capture bags, which are used for witchcraft. As you know, witchcraft is prominent in the land, and many people are used in witchcraft. The exploration of witchcraft is ancient, and its usefulness to people is so misleading. It so captivates their hearts to darkness. This black capturing bag is significant, where the realms of darkness are used for sorcery, witchcraft, Luciferianism, and Satanism.

When these black bags are presented, you can understand that there has been witchcraft at work, but the capturing of these things is easy. Angels plunder these regularly. Infiltrations of witchcraft, sorcery, Luciferianism, and Satanism will all be easily captured in these bags. Use them. They are your tools.

When you have been alerted that there have been possible infiltrations of witchcraft, sorcery, and the like, these are the tools angels will use. They will capture them. However, these bags are not for gathering plunder. Other bags are used for plunder.

———·———

Chapter 10
The Kingdom Dynamics of the Glory & Essence of the Father

A few days after seeing our first capture bag, Stephanie and I stepped into Heaven to learn some more about them. We were taken to an office, and the first thing Stephanie noticed was the color of the walls, which were golden-yellow.

Golden Glory Bags

Lydia came to instruct us. Lydia began to teach on what she called the gold glory bags. The color of the walls where we were was symbolic of how glory presents itself to the human eye. She explained that there were capturing bags and there were bags of Glory. These can be administered by the angels into people's realm.

Stephanie visualized us taking these bags and stepping into them and pulling them up around us. What Holy Spirit was showing me that we were doing was because the Glory is all encompassing. It surrounds us. These are like how we would release Godly bonds to people. It is something that we can release on behalf of people.

The Glory bags will be something that you commission their angels to bring to them.

It is a part of awakening their angels, stirring them up, and working on behalf of those that come for prayer and for ministry.

Silver Capture Bags

A few days later we were in another engagement and found ourselves back in the ballroom we had seen in a different engagement.[44] This time we were to learn about the silver bags. Malcolm was our tutor and he described how this bag was aerodynamic, but that it did not capture, rather it contained. It contains something to be released to others. It contains the essence of the Father—the essence of Holy Spirit; and what it contains will bring the evidence of that into people's lives—the essence of the Father, the strength of the Father, the goodness of the Father, the plans of the Father, the need of the Father, the value of worship of the Father, and the friendship of the

---

[44] This is discussed in *Dealing with Trusts & Consequential Liens in the Courts of Heaven*, LifeSpring Publishing (2022).

Father. These are necessary things that people have been missing in their lives. The use of these bags is also for the generations and is used in generational work.

Its usefulness is to capture the captive—those that are captive.

The Essence of the Father

Many like the simplicities and the simplistic ways that they can utilize tools of the Kingdom. That is what these bags are. People can mentally and visually speak and see these things as a helpful tool on their behalf, because of the simplicity of it. When people are praying about it, it creates a boldness, a feeling of accomplishment, a sense of the co-laboring, and that they are useful in the co-laboring with the angels. They are gaining strength from it, and they are seeing results.

These are not capturing bags in the sense most of the other bags are. These are bags that *contain* the essence—all those things mentioned above, to be given to that person. It acts like a bonding agent—like a bond. It can be a bond that is released when it is relevant and an opportune time to do so.

The usefulness of these silver bags comes when we are praying on behalf of someone, we can say (to our angels), "As an act of faith, take that silver bag to myself." Many have missed the relational side of prayer, but many can visually experience the relationship. They can physically experience the relationship of the Father as this tool is used by the body. This unsophisticated action shows the simplicity of Heaven, yet it is profound love and favor for the body and for the people. Think of it as an act of love, and in turn, your release of that on behalf of someone else is also an act of love—love for your neighbor, love for your friend, love for family, love for the Body of Christ.

Use this diligently. Use it often. The essence of the Father and His love will settle upon the people. There will be a fragrance about it—an enhancement because of it, a beauty around it, and a just cause will bear witness from it. Use this in your courtroom work. It is tangible. Its immediate effects will be known as the effective fervent prayers of a righteous man availing much.[45]

We can simply receive the silver bags into our realms. It is tangible. This is something we can release to a believer who is struggling. It is very much like how a bond works.

The definition of essence is helpful to understand. Malcolm said, "It's an entire world." We took a moment to look at the definition of "essence."[46] It is quite interesting. "The intrinsic nature or indispensable quality of something that determines its character, especially something abstract."

The philosophy definition was, "The inherent unchanging nature of a thing or class of things, especially

---

[45] James 5:16
[46] Google's English Dictionary definition of *essence*.

as contrasted with its existence," and also "a property or group of properties of something without which it would not exist or be what it is." An additional definition said, "An extract or concentrate obtained from a particular plant or other matter and used for flavoring or scent. It creates a frequency."

"The most significant element, quality, or aspect of a thing or person in concentrated form or substance as of a perfume."

"Something that exists, an entity."

Wikipedia had an interesting definition: "Essence. It's a polysomic term using philosophy and theology as a designation for the property or set of properties **that make an entity or substance what it fundamentally is** and which it has by necessity and **without which it loses its identity**."[47]

This essence, the essence of the Father, can be released using the silver bag, even for those who do not understand this prayer paradigm, even for those who need the Essence of the Father—His love, His friendship, and it will be astounding to them. They will experience a drawing near to the Father. We can simply receive the contents of the silver bag into our realms. We can see ourselves holding the Glory bag and stepping into it.

---

[47] Wikipedia definition of *essence*.

Containers to be Released

These bags are containers to be released as opposed to bags that capture things. These two bags (gold and silver) are containers of the Glory of the Father and the Essence and Love of the Father that need to be released to people. They are also containers to gather. We can utilize them to gather people into the Glory and the Essence and Love of the Father. Sometimes people who get caught up in words, when they are hearing people talk about the Glory, they have not ascertained how to utilize it for themselves. This is a simplistic, loving way that people can use their imaginations to utilize it for themselves and as they pray for others. We can also request these bags be released on behalf of LHS's. The Glory bag simply contains the Glory of God to be released to people.

Those who struggle when they hear these messages, and are falsely believing that they themselves cannot ascertain the Glory or ascertain the love and the Essence of the Father—these are great tools for them on their behalf. They *can* imagine. They *can see* whether they are a seer or not and can understand what a bag looks like, feels like, and *can* imagine themselves stepping into the Glory with the use of the tool that is the Glory bag. They *can* ascertain the essence and the experience of it with the tool that is the silver bag. Simplicity is needed at times, and at times these tools are needed.

Make skillful use of them, for they are for our benefit because of the Father's love. Because we have said yes to co-laboring with angels, this is a direct result and a benefit of that. It is a reminder that angels are not just useful in battle, but they are useful in the presentation of the Father's love and of His Glory and of His Kingdom.

We can commission angels to take the silver bags to those who have drawn near the ministry. The benefit of these bags to the people has been a great honor for the angels to deliver on behalf of those that have drawn close to the ministry and especially on behalf of those who work for the ministry. It is the Father's love.

Great benefit comes from loving the Father and choosing His Kingdom.

These are Kingdom benefits. Look at them like that. Align with the Kingdom of Heaven. As simple as this may seem, it will work profoundly in our lives.

The Essence and the Glory

As revelation unfolded, we had another engagement in which we saw a picture of what the Essence and the Glory look like together—a pure white light. The light then leapt off the table and into outer space.

We were told by Joseph, a man in white, that the Father's Glory and Essence upon the earth, upon men's hearts, and upon their realms, would be evident just as we see the flame, just as in the day when Holy Spirit came, and flames were seen above the people.[48] The essence will rest upon the people.

We were invited to walk with him, and we stopped at a brook, and referring to an engagement David, Stephanie, and I had the prior day, Joseph said, "The baptismal pool you saw is an invitation to not just to Sandhills Ecclesia,[49] but to all who draw close to the ministry, to step into the water which contains the Essence of His Glory—there will be evidence upon their lives. You will see the evidence. This is the goodness of Heaven. The early believers experienced the evidence of speaking a language heretofore unknown to them. Heaven is going to do this marvelous thing."

We were then transported back to a different room. Jason, a man in white, was present to assist us. He brought an ancient book. On the cover was a large medallion, and Jason took a sword and inserted it into the keyhole that was in the medallion, turning the sword like a key. As he did, one could hear the unlocking of the lock mechanism. The book was entitled *The Book of Numbers*. Stephanie asked if this was "a" book of numbers, or "the" [Biblical] book of Numbers. She was assured it was the latter, and it was suggested we turn to Numbers 4. Jason began helping unpack information in that passage and later in chapter 27, which spoke of

---

[48] Acts 2:3

[49] Sandhills Ecclesia is a weekly gathering of believers via Zoom to legislate in the earth. (See SandhillsEcclesia.com). This message is dated 2/27/22 and is available on the website.

inheritance. A principle of inheritance was unveiled that is simply:

> *An inheritance may be distributed,*
> *but to have benefit,*
> *it must be possessed.*

The passage in Numbers 27 spoke of those who were to carry the presence. Today, that is you and me.

We were told to tell you that each of your realms carries the tabernacle within you.[50] You are a type and shadow of the tabernacle, the holy that lives within you—the Essence AND the Glory, you carry within you. There are those that need this Essence and this Glory. It will shine and be evident upon each of you. They will see it. They will know it. They will want it and desire it.

This is confirmed in 1 Peter 2:5-7:

> *"⁵Come and be His 'living stones' who are continually being assembled into a sanctuary for God. For now, you serve as holy priests, offering up spiritual sacrifices that He readily accepts through Jesus Christ. ⁶ For it says in Scripture: Look! I lay a cornerstone in Zion, a chosen and priceless stone! And whoever believes in Him will certainly not be disappointed. ⁷ As believers you*

---

[50] 1 Corinthians 6:19 *"Have you forgotten that your body is now the sacred temple of the Spirit of Holiness, who lives in you? You don't belong to yourself any longer, for the gift of God, the Holy Spirit, lives inside your sanctuary."* (TPT); also 2 Corinthians 6:19

know His great worth—indeed, **His preciousness is imparted to you**. But for those who do not believe: The stone that the builders rejected and discarded has now become the cornerstone." (TPT) (Emphasis added)

The flame that people see upon you will be so evident that many will be drawn to it, and it will alight upon others.

This is a fulfillment of what Isaiah spoke of long ago:

"¹ Arise, shine; for your light has come! And the glory of the LORD is risen upon you. ² For behold, the darkness shall cover the earth, and deep darkness the people; but the LORD will arise over you, and His glory will be seen upon you.

From the New King James Version:

³ The Gentiles shall come to your light, and kings to the brightness of your rising. ⁴ "Lift up your eyes all around, and see: they all gather together, they come to you; your sons shall come from afar, and your daughters shall be nursed at your side. ⁵ Then you shall see and become radiant, and your heart shall swell with joy; because the abundance of the sea shall be turned to you, the wealth of the Gentiles shall come to you." (Isaiah 60:1-5) (Emphasis added)

All that we were hearing was referring to the baptism of Holy Spirit *and* fire.

> *The Essence and the Glory is what creates the fire. The fire is the Essence and the Glory combined.*

Imagine the two of them together—the gold and the silver bags. When we release these for people and on behalf of people, contained within them and combined is the fire.

> *Moses brought their case before the Lord. ⁶ And the Lord spoke to Moses saying ⁷the daughters of Zelophedad speak what is right; you shall surely give them a possession of inheritance among their father's brothers, and cause the inheritance of their father to pass to them. (Numbers 27:5)*

Just like in Numbers 27, where the Lord laid out what inheritances were for the people on our earth, this is an inheritance. This is the truest form of inheritance from the Father—His Glory and His Essence combined, bringing the fire upon the people, lighting the fire within them, dwelling upon them, and being so evident that people are drawn to the light—the flame.

In the beginning, when the Lord set up the inheritance in the natural using the Courts of Heaven, there is also an inheritance for us in the spiritual. Here it not only has to be distributed, but this inheritance also *must be possessed*. The sword of the Lord—it is your strength and Wisdom is at your right hand. The Glory and the Essence that will be upon you, bringing the fire of the Lord.

On behalf of this ministry, this was a new walk—a new beginning for the people and for the Kingdom, with new insight and new understanding—all this was gained from the seat of rest, all of it because He loves us.

Heaven said, "This flame will be evident upon you just as it is evident in my hand. As the Father releases His Glory and His Essence upon the people, and what you described as an ember will be a movement."

This is what the earth groans for. An innumerable number of angels carry this. They carry this torch. They carry this flame which is being released for such a time as this. It will grow just as a natural fire grows and will spread. This will spread. This will bring people from the north, south, east, and west.

The Commission for the Essence & the Glory[51]

I commission you, Ezekiel, in the name of Jesus, with your commanders, and ranks, on behalf of the people, those who have drawn near to the ministry and align with it,, those who work for the ministry, and their families, to bring the flame that is the Essence and the Glory of the Father upon the people, that it spread like embers and light upon the people, so that all may see that it as

---

[51] Feel free to customize this to your situation.

evidence, as the Father has said that it would be in evidence.

I commission you to the full use of the silver and the gold bags that carry the Essence and carry the Glory and to bring them to everyone's realms, in the name of Jesus.

Father, I would like for Understanding to go with this commissioning that is being released—this fire.

Father, I request that Understanding be released for all of those that hear, that draw near, that seek the Kingdom of God, and I release you, Ezekiel, your commanders, and ranks to do this good work on behalf of the Father, in Jesus' name.

I commission you to these things both in time and out of time.

With that, Ezekiel turned and left.

Welcoming Understanding

We were told that much understanding would come from this. We were to be patient. This is a new level. A new place. Understanding will come. Understanding is going to be playing a very large role at this level.

We welcomed Understanding saying, "I welcome you in everything; and just like I hold Wisdom's hand, I want to hold your hand."

There are new frequencies being released upon the earth through these messages; frequencies that are so supernatural, that Understanding being released upon them is what is going to bring this understanding of this frequency to their ears. Just like the flame and the embers, you will see it grow among the people quickly.

———·———

Chapter 11
The Kingdom Dynamics of Plunder, Defense, & Frequencies

Continuing the prior engagement, the room suddenly changed colors to green. Ezekiel explained, "These are the plunder bag colors. The green represents the wealth, and the sevenfold return of things stolen. *We can use them in tandem as we plunder the kingdoms of darkness.*"

Green Capture Bags

We were told that we were to receive this information because the Father loves the authority that we stand in and the co-laboring with angels that we do. The Angels of the Hosts have not been nearly as active as Heaven wants them to be, but the saints are awakening to them and their work. He gives this information because He loves this—the awakening of His children, the hunger for knowledge, the hunger for Heaven, the hunger for Him. It is His great pleasure. It is His joy.

The lessons in leaning in our paradigms of prayer was for when we call upon the angels to use these capturing bags during times of attack, especially the release of the Glory bags for the people. They work in tandem when we call upon the angels to silence the principalities. The end-product of this is the usefulness with the angels, the co-laboring with the saints, and the use of the capturing bags, including the Glory bags and the silver bags. They produce a quick silencing of the enemy and the opening of the Kingdom Dynamics of Heaven.

Your realms, who you are, how God created you, your arche that you will learn about,[52] which also includes mountains—even things you don't understand—it is a landscape, which is why the principalities consider it a region and why it can be impacted by a consequential lien.[53]

Your footsteps on the earth create your region upon the earth.

We were shown a brilliantly shining bright orb hovering over the table in the conference room. On the

---

[52] Arche is discussed in Chapter 28.
[53] Consequential liens are discussed in *Dealing with Trusts & Consequential Liens in the Courts of Heaven*, LifeSpring Publishing (2022).

table were four books: the Book of LifeSpring, the Book of Sandhills Ecclesia, the Book of CourtsNet, and the BAS Global[54] Book were on the table. The orb was the light of what was coming. As the orb came closer to the table, it grew in mass. It hovered above all four books. Power was going into *all* the books but was also hovering above them. We were told it was knowledge, integrity, wisdom—a lightning-force swift action upon the hearts of man that come into this teaching. It was Kingdom Dynamics, because we pray "Your Kingdom come, Your will be done." It was His ultimate will. That's what this orb was—His will. We were told we could think of it in those terms. Many aspects to what we were seeing came out of this as His will. It is because the Kingdom is at hand.

We came to understand that because of obedience, prayer, and all the things Heaven had been showing us, that His will was evident in all four of the books. It is a pouring out of all those things mentioned in those books that will affect the people as it reflects the ministry, which reflects His will because of praying for His Kingdom to come.[55]

Everyone one who had joined us began leaving the room, but the books were still open. We were shown that another book was coming. We had seen the books for

---

[54] BAS (Business Advocate Services), now known as Heaven Down Business, is an extension of LifeSpring.
[55] For years I have prayed, "Come Kingdom of God, be done will of God" in my daily prayer life.

LifeSpring, CourtsNet, BAS Global, and Sandhills Ecclesia, but the new book was more darkened and not opened yet. Apparently, its content is still to be unveiled.

The Commissioning[56]

I call Ezekiel, his commanders, and his ranks, along with my angels to come near. Father, I request on behalf of the angels, all the different sizes, classifications, and colors of every capturing bag needed to serve the Kingdom of Heaven and to serve your people, in Jesus' name.

Ezekiel, I commission you, your commanders, and your ranks to use the classifications of every capturing bag needed to go and capture the infiltrations, to use the different colors and classifications of the bags as needed from the smallest demon to the largest domain, in the name of Jesus.

I also request of the Father Glory bags for distribution to the saints hearing this message as well as silver bags.

I commission you to the full use of these gold Glory bags and the silver bags for the Glory of the Father in the lives of His sons and daughters, in Jesus' name.

---

[56] Feel free to adapt this commissioning to your situation.

Angels are free to use capture bags for anything that is illegally in place. However, if something has a legal right to be in place, they cannot capture that. Repentance is necessary in order to remove the legal rights of the enemy in that arena. Again, repentance is key to the full working of the angels and capture bags.

Blue Capture Bags

We had seen blue capture bags but had no understanding of them. We were desiring instruction about the blue capture bags, which typically appeared much smaller—more of a regular size than some other Capture Bags we had seen. Malcolm explained to us that the blue bags capture the enemy's weapons.

Satan is a legalist, but he is also a copycat. His falsehood represents weaponry, as we would in the natural think of weaponry, but his weapons *are only tactics*. This has perplexed us in that, in the natural, we think of him attacking us with weapons. His weapons are *words* and *lies—tactical strategies of deception*. The blue bags capture the paradigms that perplex us.

When it comes to the enemy's warfare and talking about arrows, your armor will deflect the arrows from the enemy. We may have always assumed they were actual weapons. We saw them as actual arrows, but words or strategies can inflict more damage than a natural arrow ever could upon a person's realms. Capture the accusations! In this paradigm, you don't have to get caught up in saying, 'Angels, go and capture the words and the phrases and the strategies.' Sending a blue bag will capture all of that and more. You can also say, 'Capture the accusations.' You can do that before the enemy has a legal right to bring it to the Courts of Heaven against you. This is the sovereignty of God on behalf of His sons.

Picture Jacob's ladder and how the accuser ascends and descends a ladder to bring accusations against us. Sometimes, the enemy comes to us personally, speaking to us about where to accuse ourselves or about where we accuse others in our hearts and our mind.

To make an accusation is not a sin, until we embrace it and we act upon it."

This can be done to prevent those words and accusations of the enemy from reaching our spirit and our heart and our soul. Our repentance is for the entertaining of these accusations against others and against ourselves, et cetera. Before the enemy can take an accusation to the Courts of Heaven to accuse you and where you must come into agreement with the accuser, *the step before that* is when you come into agreement—you hear it, and you take it on. That is when he can have a legal right to accuse you.

> *The blue capture bags are a part*
> *of the paradigms of prayer*
> *to forfeit the enemy's legal right*
> *to form accusations against us.*

This is a gift from the Father. This bag is for His sovereignty towards us, in that if we can utilize this commissioning of the angels, it is a prevention of the next step of the enemy against us, which is where we would come into agreement or take on the accusation. It circumvents that for us *because we are His children*. The Father is the one who has simplified this aspect, so we are not dealing with accusations over and over repeatedly. Heaven is simply taking that out of the equation for us. Look how the Father loves. That is what this is. He is giving you this tool. It's like a preventative medicine.

> *It is for dismantling something*
> *before it begins. It's a preventative.*

People have just been sick and tired of the same accusations over and over repeatedly. This tool is something we can use in our paradigms of prayer as we commission angels to use this on our behalf, where we are not accepting or falling for the enemy's tactics, but instead are being given Kingdom tactics that are offensive not defensive. It is for us, preventative measures.

Hand in Hand with Wisdom

Wisdom appeared with a large iridescent pearl in her hand. She was turning it in her hand and reminded us that she had given us the Wisdom of Ages a few days before. She instructed us to tell the people to invoke her. She said to invoke Wisdom in *everything* that we do and in all the teachings that are being taught. If we come to her door, we can request Wisdom, we can request the angels to use the capture bags along with the extraordinary things that LifeSpring brings to people, and that she will give them the Wisdom of Ages.

It is the Father's desire that you carry Wisdom—the Pearls of Wisdom, around your neck. She then set a large Pearl of Wisdom on the table in front of me and said, "It is yours for the keeping. It's the continuing of the Wisdom of Ages. As I teach you, I want you to teach the people that Wisdom must be invoked—she must be invited. It is necessary."

Walking Together

Ezekiel then appeared, demonstrating how he and Wisdom walk together through things. He was demonstrating that as we teach the people about Wisdom—about the need to understand that using Wisdom and all these things, including arming your angels and co-laboring with your angels—that walking with the entity Wisdom is an important piece of the puzzle.

He has showed us that he and Wisdom were holding hands, and that's how he wants the people to see themselves: as holding hands with Wisdom and Wisdom holding hands with Ezekiel. This is also a representation of their own personal angels who should be commissioned to walk hand in hand with Wisdom. It's a three-cord strand.

He smiled and began to walk away hand-in-hand with Wisdom. In his other hand he slung an orange bag over his shoulder.

> [6] *"Wisdom is a gift from a generous God, and every word Wisdom speaks is full of revelation and becomes a fountain of understanding within you.*
>
> [9] *"Then you will discover all that is just, proper, and fair, and be empowered to make the right decisions as you walk into your destiny.*
>
> [10] *"When Wisdom wins your heart and revelation breaks in, true pleasure enters your soul."*
> *(Proverbs 2:6, 9, 10 TPT)*

Grey Capture Bags

Jeremy, one of our team members, was in prayer recently in response to a request for how to deal with a situation he was facing in his home. Jeremy and his wife parent several small children, and he noticed some movies or television shows were releasing a lot of profanity into the air which was polluting the atmosphere. He heard Heaven say, "Request Grey Capture Bags."

Asking what the grey bags did, he heard, "The Grey Capture Bags work much like a shop vac or leaf blower that has both sucking and blowing capabilities—they have dual use. When requesting the Grey Capture Bags, essentially your angels will be able to kill two birds with one stone."

Heaven said, "The **first component is the isolation and removal of any ungodly frequencies.**" He could see an angel holding a bag that was fully inflated and it was sucking in all the ungodly frequencies in the space in front and around of where the bag was positioned.

Heaven continued, **"The second feature is the release of Godly frequencies and the frequency of Heaven."**

Again, he could see the angel with the bag, only this time a golden sparkling mist was being released.

Jeremy's angel said, "It basically has dual-action cleaning power." His angel chuckled and then showed him how the ungodly frequencies can suck the life and joy out of an atmosphere and leave the people in that atmosphere feeling heavy or agitated.

Jeremy saw the scene depicting this as a vivid image that had all the color sucked out of it. The individuals in the image looked very melancholy, but when the Godly frequencies were released, it was like a revival breaking out. Suddenly the color reappeared, more vibrant than before, and everyone seemed alive with the joy of the Lord. There was also a serenity and a peace that came over the scene with the release of these Godly frequencies.

Jeremy sensed the need to request and commission his angels to use this new item for his house and family.

Father, in Jesus' name, I request the Grey Capture Bags for our angels and ranks, and I commission our angels to use these bags to remove the ungodly frequencies and release the heavenly frequencies into our home and realms, in Jesus' name.

He asked, "Can these be used in tandem with other frequency weapons like shields and headphones. He heard, "Yes."

He asked, "Are they specifically for the frequencies of words and sound waves and again he heard, "Yes."

Adding the Grey Capture Bags to the tool kit of Heaven known as Capture Bags should help the Body of Christ gain new levels of freedom. Enjoy them! Use them!

———·———

Chapter 12
The Kingdom Dynamics of Overcoming Domains & Dominions

Orange was the color for today. As Ezekiel was walking away in a prior engagement, we noticed he was carrying an orange bag over his shoulder.

Orange Capture Bags

Asking what it was about, Ezekiel paused and said, "It's for domains. **Orange is the capturing of a domain.** Domains are evil empires-evil domains. I used it in conjunction with the Purple bag. (We could see purple bag inside of the orange bag.) This domain that I captured was in another time and dimension."

Ezekiel had captured a domain— one that was encroaching upon the ministry that was being built by the enemy to create an illusion to other people—a false domain. Someone was trying to create a false domain to be a replica—a duplicate of LifeSpring Ministries, but he captured it. Remember, he takes these and destroys them and the bags. He would be taking this orange bag to destroy it. The domain Ezekiel spoke of was two-fold. (1) The domain where someone was going to duplicate or create a false replica of LifeSpring Ministries, where when people go to a search of LifeSpring, they were going to be taken to a different place. It was the false domain in the natural as well as (2) a domain in the spiritual—a room where it was created in a different dimension in time.

We thanked him for the capture, and he disclosed that the strategy for that capture had come from the Strategy Room. He knew from the Strategy Room where to go to capture this domain in time and out of time, as well as taking down that platform.

We again thanked Ezekiel as he walked away having taught us even more about capture bags and the various colors.

Brown Capture Bags

Earlier in the day, I mentioned to Stephanie that I wanted to learn more about capture bags and more about what certain colors meant. We stepped into the realms of Heaven, asking for a meeting with Malcolm. He was waiting for us in the classroom with an eraser and two pieces of chalk in his hand.

When he asked what we wanted to learn about today, we responded with an answer that we felt he already knew. We wanted to know about the different color bags.

We heard the word "aerodynamic."

Malcolm told us we heard the word aerodynamic for a reason. It is their usefulness. In the natural, when something is aerodynamic, it goes faster. Malcolm then began drawing on the whiteboard. He drew a big bag. The larger he drew it, the larger the whiteboard became. He became small in comparison. As he was drawing on the whiteboard, we could see the rope with which angels tie capture bags. It was a very large bag. He was going to talk to us about size and color simultaneously. With that, Malcolm began coloring the bag brown.

Dominions on Land

We learned that this brown bag **captures land that was taken captive by the enemy.** It is essentially 'illegal land,' or land under an illegal ownership claim.

The vision we saw was of land taken captive by the enemy that belongs to the children of God—the sons of God. It was like a dominion but was not a dominion. This was taking captive a dominion that has been encamped and where the enemy had encroached upon the land. It was like a territory, but unlike the domains which can be captured in the Orange Bag, it is different from that because this one deals with physical earth. In the situation we were seeing, it was the result of a consequential lien that a principality put upon a region of land or someone's land that was stolen. This was an encroaching of an evil dominion upon land.

We then saw where natural land had been cursed by the bloodshed that occurred on it, and the land had been stolen. The legal right was two-fold—the shedding of innocent blood and the theft of the land. These gave the legal right to the principality to overlay an evil dominion on someone's territory or land mass in the natural.

Remember the account in the book of Daniel about princes being over regions—like the Prince of Persia being over a region that was an entire land mass. It contained an entire body of people. The freedom from the principality is for individuals' sakes and for families' sakes. This pertains to land that has been stolen from people, even in the natural. Think of it as the land that the Native Americans had stolen from them. An evil dominion has been placed over them and their heritage—an evil dominion that can be easily captured and dismantled.

Repentance work that has already been done concerning land that has been taken like that can be applied for the capture bags by simply commissioning the angels to retrieve the land and remove the captured principality. Other repentance work may also be needed. Be led of Holy Spirit in that arena.

The ability to remove the principality is a part of the parameter[57] and will be a useful tool when dealing with parameters that are seen on someone's life as a trust. The Godly trust in this is all that Heaven has for us, including inheritances that were stolen from us—which includes land.

Stephanie desired an illustration of what Malcolm was telling us. She began to see Kevin (one of our Senior Advocates) doing courtroom work and looking at someone's Trust Registry, realizing that there is a parameter and a consequential lien that has been placed upon land that has been stolen geographically and people groups who live on that land. She exclaimed, "He is showing it to me as masses of people, and I keep seeing Native Americans specifically."

In the vision, we saw was a land mass—an actual natural land mass. We saw a coastline and a castle on a hill overlooking the ocean. We saw the whole land mass captured, then we saw the evil domain overlaying the captured land mass. The purpose of this brown capture bag, used in conjunction with removal of consequential liens, is to capture the dominion and free the land mass. "Is it that easy to capture the dominion?" we asked Malcolm.

"Well, yes! This IS Heaven!" he exclaimed.

---

[57] Parameters are discussed in-depth in my book *Dealing with Trusts & Consequential Liens in the Courts of Heaven*, LifeSpring Publishing (2022).

Instead of dealing with little peon demons, we are dealing with principalities and getting it over with. We are just now beginning to understand the magnitude of the finished work of Jesus with the simplicity of what we have as sons of God, because of His finished work and His blood that was shed. This is the work of Heaven and the Kingdom Dynamics.

How does this work in relation to cities?

There are evil dominions who have taken over land masses and cities. Remember the Prince of Persia. As we are doing this work with the capture bags that are given to the angels it is like what was used by the angel that visited Daniel. That is what was used then and that is what will be used now—a brown capture bag.

Imagine individual capture bags that are brown related to every state of the United States. Imagine looking at each state in the natural and then see in the spirit the overlay of the evil dominion over each state, city, or town. Now see the bloodshed that has occurred over them. That is how the dominion can take authority.

One of the first things to look at concerning the legal right a prince exercises is innocent bloodshed, followed by profane worship, and all the things you've been taught related to this. That is why that information was the forerunner of understanding to this paradigm now.

Dominions on the Seas

Not only do we have evil dominions over land but also over the seas. Envision the bloodshed on ships, some of whom were slaves or died in war, ships that went down into the seas which were related to the work of water kingdoms, and where the dominion had captured LHS's in that place. The work would be two-fold: dealing with the principality through repentance for the bloodshed, et cetera, and helping the LHS's get free, transitioning to Heaven.

We had a recent example of that when we did some repentance work for bloodshed in Mississippi and on the Mississippi River. David Porter had seen a piece of the Mississippi river open and hundreds of LHS's set free. There is a correlation of dominions to water kingdoms that needs to be understood.

We asked if Malcom had more to discuss about the brown capture bags. He showed Stephanie a picture of a little child trying to tie their shoelaces. It might take a few moments at first, but eventually you become very skilled at it. He said, "The work and the simplicity of tying a shoelace is the simplicity of this work."

Capturing Dominions

Stephanie could then see the brown capture bags. They were brought into the conference room and on these bags was written "Vital Work" in white stitching on the brown bags.

The capture of dominions is vital work.

Remember its simplicity. There will be detailed information given during times of prayer, corporate prayer, prayer over cities and nations, intercessory prayer where the full use of these vital works of capturing dominions will be used. There will be great freedom, atmospheric changes, landscape changes, mass movement—movement that is twofold—like a massive group of people moving and then the movement as an earthquake would bring to the shifting of land.

This is no light matter, but it is simplistic. Heaven will instruct because the power of the blood and the final work of Jesus have created this for mankind. The groaning of the earth has called out for such a time as this.

The Mass Release of LHS's

In a brief vision, some of what we saw was on land, and when the brown capture bags were utilized, a freeing of LHS's that had been trapped in that evil dominion occurred. Hundreds and thousands can be freed through this work. There is a streamlining to that process for the mass release of LHS's which involves the use of the brown capture bags for dominions. The dominions have held them and have traded on them. The dominions have inflicted a seizure upon them.

Stephanie saw a vision of a massive angel with a brown capture bag. He flew down with the bag and captured a dominion in it. Whereas before, it appeared as if a dark film had been over the landscape, suddenly light came breaking through. It produced an atmospheric change that allowed the release of LHS's that had been in captivity, because when you capture the dominion, you are not capturing the souls of people or the spirits of people, you are capturing the demonic principality. Yet, you are also freeing the LHS's and the souls or spirits of people that were captive within that dominion.

The simplicity is in the capture.

The complexity is in knowing when and how to commission the angels. We were reminded of a recent scene like what we experienced with the Sandhills Ecclesia as we did courtroom work concerning Mississippi and Canada. At that time, David saw a segment of the Mississippi River with LHS's coming out of it and going through the silver channel. It will seem tedious at first, but it will become very natural to you to do this.

Someone again illustrated by showing a child learning to tie their shoe. At first it seemed difficult, but after some practice it became second nature. You can do it without even thinking about it.

We could perceive that everyone we had seen during this engagement was very well pleased. They are glad that this work is going to be done.

We had seen many Warrior Angels outside the window of the conference room who were capturing angels. They are part of this work. They are simply waiting to be deployed, and they are waiting with great anticipation.

A passage of Scripture came to mind from Romans 8:

[18] I am convinced that any suffering we endure is less than nothing compared to the magnitude of glory that is about to be unveiled within us. [19] The entire universe is standing on tiptoe, yearning to see the unveiling of God's glorious sons and daughters!

[20] For against its will the universe itself has had to endure the empty futility resulting from the consequences of human sin. But now, with eager expectation, [21] all creation longs for freedom from its slavery to decay and to experience with us the wonderful freedom coming to God's children. [22] To this day we are aware of the universal agony and groaning of creation, as if it were in the contractions of labor for childbirth. [23] And it's not just creation. We who have already experienced the first fruits of the Spirit also inwardly groan as we passionately long to experience our full status as God's sons and daughters—including our physical bodies being transformed.

²⁴ For this is the hope of our salvation. But hope means that we must trust and wait for what is still unseen. For why would we need to hope for something we already have? ²⁵ So because our hope is set on what is yet to be seen, we patiently keep on waiting for its fulfillment. (Romans 8: 18-25) (TPT)

What this brown capture bag means when we see it are those things where our sin brought us into the captivity—that includes lingering spirits and their activity. We were in awe because we were seeing this ancient text played out now!

Our obedience in the toughness of the LHS book release when we walked through what could have been fear as we released that book—the consequence of that will be the mass release of LHS's as people walk in this and co-labor with Heaven and with angels. There had to be a beginning.

Tan Capture Bags

We need not assume the possibility that there is every color of bag available to do different things in the spirit. There are some colors we may not yet ever know what the color is, but the usefulness of the bags is available on behalf of the people's angels to have full use of. There are dynamics of the use of every bag.

The bag Ezekiel was now holding looked like camel hair, a tan color. It was explained that angels use them in *correlation with* the domain bags (orange bags) and in *conjunction with* the domain bags. They are very specific to domains, not in an inclusive way of just what we think of as domains within websites, but domains of the enemy. There is treachery in domains and heresy in domains.

This bag does not so much capture, rather it is used to lay down upon the treachery, upon the heresy that is in those domains, covering it. Think of it as a trampling. Angels lay them down and use them in that manner. The usefulness of it is a trampling upon the domains as they go and capture domains, they lay it down, ahead of the treachery or on top of the treachery. Angels lay it on the treachery and the heresy. The heresy Ezekiel was speaking of is an actual, tangible thing—not just a word or a deed. Heresies create structures.

Angels trample down the heresy and the treachery with the use of the tan capture bags.

This can clearly be applied where occultism is involved. The foundation of occultism is heresy. It is treachery. The bags provide a covering where our feet can land securely as we go into a place as a conquering son. As we've read in the Bible, where our feet tread upon the adder and the lion, and our feet tread upon the serpent and the snake,[58] this is like that!

When there is a snake, a recommendation is to throw a blanket over it or throw something over it and stomp on it. That is what Stephanie saw Ezekiel do! Ezekiel reminded us that the understanding of these bags is for our purposes to know *what* they are conquering. It is a way in which we can understand how the commissioning can be done.

> *I commission that these bags be laid out before you as you tread upon the lion and the adder, as you tread upon the scorpion and the snake, for these to be laid out before you as you co-labor. As you walk in the victories, that are the full use of this tool, Ezekiel.*
>
> *Ezekiel, I commend you to the Father. You, your ranks, and your commanders, and I commission you, your commanders, and ranks with the full use of this bag, to lay it down before the people, to lay it down upon the treachery—upon the heresy. As I move forward, co-laboring with you, I can walk and tread upon the lion and the adder, to tread upon the scorpion and the snake; to tread upon those things with victory, commissioning you to do this in full use of all the other bags, in time and out of time, and in every realm and*

---

[58] Psalm 91:13

dimension. I seal this with the blood of Jesus and the Sword of the Lord. I thank you.

I thank You, Father, that You keep showing me how You go before me, preparing every way.

Purple Capture Bags

Purple was the color of the capture bag we would be learning about in this engagement with Heaven.

We noted a change in the wall color as we had in other engagements. This time they switched to purple—a deep purple. It was very beautiful, and it had flashes of light through it, all over the walls like there were mirrors on the walls reflecting light. This deep royal purple was the next step down from the red capture bags. The purple bag goes into *dimensions*. It is what is needed and useful when going into other times and dimensions. It prevents what is captured from escaping when angels are taking them out of other times and dimensions. It is lined with the authority that is interwoven into the fabric of the bag, but it is a grid. It is a very useful tool. Ezekiel told us they will be doing many things *in time and out of time*, and this is the purpose of this specific capturing bag.

When we commission our angels, we are to use the full commissioning of requesting a capturing bag of every size, color, and dimension. We were rapidly progressing in our understanding of how to commission our angels concerning the capture bags.

The blood is upon all the bags, the name above all names, and the authority of that name is upon all of them. The colors are for our knowledge and understanding. We will see them play out as we work in this paradigm of prayer using these capturing bags. We will know specifically when angels come with a specific color bag what has been captured, whether it is an infiltration, whether it's black for witchcraft, or whether it is this deep, royal purple which is where something was caught in a different time, age, and dimension for our knowledge. This is the wisdom of Heaven, and because of the Father's love for us, He wants us to know all these things.

———·———

Chapter 13
The Kingdom Dynamics of Regained Innocence

Stephanie and I had engaged Heaven and we were in a boardroom with Malcolm. We had questions about some of the colors of bags others had seen and had asked me about.

Pink Capture Bags

On the whiteboard, Malcolm drew a pink bag and said it was for capturing innocence that has been stolen. This, too, is an *in time and out of time* revelation. Just as a newborn arrives with innocence, and the purity that that brings within a newborn, there is still deep corruption in the DNA and RNA, even at birth (even though they appear innocent). That is why this is used in time and out of time.

> *The innocence that was stolen in the generational line can be brought to bear.*

It can be restored to the person or to the family line. As angels bring the innocence that was stolen back into the heavenly realms—as people step into Heaven, Innocence will greet them.

The vision we had was of Innocence as a piece of themselves greeting them and enveloping them, restoring the innocence that was taken from them—from their RNA and from their DNA. It becomes as a covering upon their realms—like a garment.

The reason this is given in Heaven is because this is where Innocence stands.

> *And He chose us to be His very own, joining us to Himself even before He laid the foundation of the universe! Because of His great love, He ordained us, so that we would be seen as holy in His eyes with **an unstained innocence**. (Ephesians 1:4 TPT) (Emphasis added)*

It brings wholeness back to their soul or their spirit as a covering.

> [19] *"For God is satisfied to have all His fullness dwelling in Christ.* [20] *And by the blood of His cross, everything in Heaven and earth is brought back to Himself—back to its original intent, **restored to***

> ***innocence again!*** *²¹ ⁽²¹⁻²²⁾ Even though you were once distant from Him, living in the shadows of your evil thoughts and actions, **He reconnected you back to Himself**. He released His supernatural peace to you through the sacrifice of His own body as the sin-payment on your behalf so that you would dwell in His presence. And now there is nothing between you and Father God, for He sees you as holy, flawless, and restored....* (Colossians 1:19-22 TPT)

Someone steps into Heaven who has asked for this innocence to be brought back to them or to a family member. When they step into Heaven, it is like they are greeted by it. Stephanie saw a greeting like, "Hello, Stephanie!" and an acknowledgement. "Hello, Innocence." It became like a garment. It was put on like a robe over their whole being.

Restoring Innocence

What is the procedure to use this for restoring innocence?

Repentance for the generational line for participating or being a part of the corruption that steals the innocence—the stolen innocence from the ages.

If it is our spirit man in Heaven and Innocence greets us there, this is the truest understanding of living spirit forward. Our spirit man wears Innocence as a garment and brings it to the soul and to the body. *It is a calling of it back to us* with the understanding that it is because of the finished work—the complete work—that Jesus did that we can call back the innocence of our RNA and DNA. We can bring it from our spirit man to our soul, then it comes to the body. It is a co-laboring of our spirit man, with our soul and our body, too. Heaven has perfected what co-laboring means. They have been showing us over the last while the co-laboring of the angels with us.

Recently, they have shown us the co-laboring that will be between us and each other as we walk through this.

Heaven is revealing the co-laboring of our spirit, soul, and body. This is a labor of love from the Father.

In doing this on behalf of our generations, as we do this work with Freemasonry, Mithraism, and other things, with calling this Innocence back to ourselves, how will this affect the next generation?

This is part of the finished work of Jesus.

As we walk through the realms of Heaven, we can do this on behalf of people with the authority that we carry.

We can stir up someone's spirit man that is asleep. All the downloads from Heaven, from the Godly bonds that are released upon people's realms are, in fact, a stirring up of spirits who are asleep. We have seen the evidence of that.

We *are* intercessors when we pray on behalf of our families and those in our families that are asleep spiritually. As we have been releasing Godly bonds for them, and it has awakened their spirits. This is the same principle.

What are earmarks of the loss of innocence in people?"

The earmarks are in their DNA, the simple fact that we're born. That is the number one ear marker. *All* our Innocence has been stolen in some way.

The heart of the Father is to continually be restoring humanity back into Himself.

The tools—this revelation—these are taking away the hindrances that have been upon the hearts and minds through the spirit of religion. These are effective. They are effective in intercessory work. They are effective when we pray for our family. Use these effectively. Remember, the color of the bags is for our understanding of what we can capture or what we can release. It is just one of the tools.

Commission for the Pink Capture Bags[59]

We have seen two capture bags that are in time and out of time—purple and pink. As we are doing this work, we may see where pink capture bags are utilized.

I call my angels near, and I call Ezekiel, his commanders, and his ranks near.

I am requesting that you, in the name of Jesus, use the pink bags to capture and bring back from the very beginning—from the hand of the Father to now—the Innocence that has been stolen throughout the generations.

I repent on behalf of my generations for agreeing with the enemy that took away and stole the Innocence all the way back to the garden, even to the hand of the Father, and that corrupted my DNA and RNA.

I request that this be brought back to my realms for my spirit, in the name of Jesus.

Once someone has stood in the realms of Heaven and had their Innocence restored, they will be handed a garment—a garment of Innocence. We put it on, and speak to our soul, "Soul, do not be a gatekeeper. Accept this garment of Innocence. It has been given as a gift from the Father. Body, accept this garment of Innocence

---

[59] Feel free to adapt this to your situation and your own angels.

as it begins to reconstruct my DNA and RNA, in Jesus' name."

We then decided to do the same for a friend we shall call Robin. Stephanie said,[60]

> *I call Robin's angels near to co-labor with Ezekiel, his commanders, and ranks with my angels. I commission you to go back in time and out of time on behalf of Robin, as we repent on behalf of the generations for partnering with and for being a part of the Innocence stolen that has affected the DNA and the RNA all the way back to the hand of the Father.*
>
> *I commission you to bring back the Innocence that has been stolen.*
>
> *I call Robin's spirit into heavenly realms to have the garment of Innocence placed upon her. I speak to Robin's spirit to teach the soul not to be a gatekeeper, to accept and receive this, and to bring this Innocence into her body, to change her DNA and RNA back to the Innocence that the Father designed in His original plan for us, in Jesus' name.*

Aren't we glad that Innocence can be brought back to the body? Many people will struggle with this concept because they have divulged themselves into false understanding that the Father cannot restore innocence

---

[60] Feel free to adapt this to your situation.

that has been stolen. This is related to that Scripture where they believe in godliness, but not the power of it.[61]

I was reminded of a testimony I heard of a woman who had been a prostitute. She got born again, and it was important to her to have her innocence restored. She just cried to the Lord for that. Sometime later, she ended up getting remarried and on her wedding night, her sheets were bloody. Her innocence had been restored.

We talked a few moments of how important this is for children whose innocence was stolen by others, for those who have been involved in sex trafficking or similar things. Having Innocence restored can go a long way to wholeness for them, and Heaven has obliged us with a simple way to see Innocence restored.

Malcolm reminded us that even though we do not have a full understanding of how this works, it is all done in the spirit realm. We simply need to accept all that Heaven has. The pink bag was the only bag that was used as we stepped into Heaven. That is because of the purity there. That is where the innocence is put upon us, and it is brought into our realms.

The Angel Purity

Innocence and the Angel Purity co-labor. Purity has longed with the heart of the Father regarding Innocence

---

[61] 2 Timothy 3:5

for people—Innocence and purity. The completion of their work is that they are one.

> *As an act of faith, when I step into Heaven, I ask for the Innocence to be brought back to me. I accept and put on the robe of it. Purity's job—the work that I am choosing to allow her to do as I bring Innocence to my realms, to my spirit, soul, and body—is the knitting together of my being.*
>
> *I commission you, Purity, to take my garment of Innocence that I have received in Heaven and to knit it to my soul and to my body, in Jesus' name.*

These commissions are part of the redeeming because of how they release our angels to work.

I remarked about something I had learned from Joseph Sturgeon,[62] that Purity had worked with Noah when it was said, *"He was made perfect in his generations."*[63] Purity worked with Noah and his DNA to remove the spots. Noah understood iniquity in the generations because the Lord had revealed that to him. Because he stepped into Heaven and received his innocence and because he forgave his ancestors, he did what looked like courtroom work on behalf of his generations. This was part of the restoration of his innocence and the restoration of his DNA and RNA.

---

[62] *Treasures of Darkness, Volume 2: Echoes of the Father* by Joseph C. Sturgeon II, Seraph Creative (2016).

[63] Genesis 6:9

Moses, when he was on the mountain, and as he was coming down his face shone so brightly that they had to cover his face. The only reason it happened in the natural is because there was restoration to his soul and his body of the innocence that had been stolen, which in turn brought the knitting of that innocence to his soul and his body because of her work.

> *When there is innocence there is purity.*

They all live in the same house together. They are one in that sense, because without corruption, when there's true Innocence the way the Father created us to be, there is purity.

Purity then showed how Eve, even though she was deceived and ate of the fruit, lost her purity. She still had Innocence, but Adam lost both at the same time when he ate of the fruit. In a sense, Innocence is something we wear. That is why it can be easily discarded when we sin, but it is also how it is corrupted in generations.

Capture Bag Commission[64]

Now that we have read about the various capture bags, I thought it would be appropriate to provide a template for commissioning our angels regarding the use

---

[64] Feel free to adapt this to your situation.

of capture bags (making sure to be in repentance of anything as needed, being led by the Holy Spirit, so the capture bags are efficient).

I call the angels assigned to me to come near.

Father, I request on behalf of these angels, all the different sizes, classifications, and colors of every capture bag needed to serve the Kingdom of Heaven and to serve your people, in Jesus' name.

I commission the angels assigned to me to use every classification, size, and color of capturing bag needed; to go and capture the infiltrations; to use the different colors and classifications of the bags as needed from the smallest demon to the largest domain, in the name of Jesus; to use these capturing bags throughout my realms and those of my family.

I commission you to network and cooperate with Ezekiel, his commanders, and ranks and to work with the Bond Registry angels, in Jesus' name.

Chapter 14
The Kingdom Dynamics of Safety & Security

This engagement with Heaven started out with an interesting scene. We were in a large golden ballroom with large giant balls bouncing around with people inside them. Like the human hamster balls that we can get inside and roll around without getting hurt. Malcolm was present and laughing at the sight. We, of course, had questions.

Malcolm asked if we would like another Lesson in Leaning (this time spelled 'leaning' instead of 'liening' as we had seen in prior engagements) and as if we were leaning upon each other.

Explanation came as the concept of the bouncing balls is profound, yet simplistic. Many in the Body of Christ feel like they have been bouncing around from one place to another, from one ministry to another, from one hopelessness to another, one flavor of understanding after another. This could even be through other religions. People have been searching. Some have been pining away in the dark, not knowing where to go.

The bouncing balls in the ballroom look like fun and are in a place that is safe. The balls are not going to run away or run out into the street. The people are in a place that feels free, but also secure. This is what people have been seeking for, a place where they find freedom and a place of security. This is the Father's Kingdom. This is Kingdom Dynamics. These balls represent people. The Father's heart is that they are not bouncing around in the world from one place to another, but their hearts and minds are free in the Father's Kingdom to bounce things off one another, to be at play in their heart, in their minds with one another.

What the Father is bringing to the body will bring this joy, this freedom, and this security. There is security and secureness in Him, and He will bring it to each of us. Then we will show one another this freedom and this security. People will see it. They will feel it. They will hear it. They will understand it from one another. We are in unison. We are in unity. We are in security.

Trust of Trust

The lesson here is Trust of Trust. It is how people will experience the Trust of Trust. They will trust the Father. They will trust this Kingdom Dynamic. There will be security in it. They will feel it. Not many people have experienced that kind of security with other people within a ministry, but Heaven is showing us that that is what this will be. That is what this is—freedom, unity, security in the Father's Kingdom.

The scenery then changed, and we found ourselves in the conference room. Wisdom was present, and she stepped forward to where we were sitting at the conference table. She called us by name saying, "Stephanie and Ron, because you have chosen to invoke me in this work and on behalf of the Body of Christ and you have told the body the value that Wisdom brings to the table, there is an extension to the provision that is Wisdom."

When we are trusted,
we will be <u>en</u>trusted.

There is more, so much more that the Kingdom of Heaven is bringing to light. It is also a part of the *Trust of Trust* that you are walking in with the Father and the Kingdom of Heaven. Expect more! Expect greater! Expect!

Chapter 15
The Kingdom Dynamics of Constructive Trusts

As our Senior Advocates began to implement the revelation of the consequential liens and trusts,[65] more information began to be revealed. Joyce Ruck Poupart, one of our Senior Advocates with a solid track record in helping advocate for people in the Courts of Heaven, received very interesting and powerful insight into what Heaven referred to as a Constructive Trust.

Here is what she wrote to me:

The trust created blinders over the group, in terms of a mindset, and had become a blanket of strife on them. This had to be removed along with consequential liens which served as parameters.

---

[65] This is taught in my book, *Dealing with Trusts & Consequential Liens in the Courts of Heaven*, LifeSpring Publishing (2022).

I requested that the angels come in with all necessary bags—brown for principalities and powers, dominions and territories that had been established, black for witchcraft, red for infiltration, orange for domains, and blue for accusations.

The definition she received from the Father was:

A constructive trust involves a trade from Heaven of the highest order. It is not like a bond from man to God, but a Constructive Trust comes from God to man. It is from the Father. It becomes a domain, collapsing the frequency and foundation of the former trusts, liens, and consequential liens. It is a trade of My Word, My power, and the Anointing of My Spirit which trumps what Satan and his emissaries have done. It becomes an establishing platform to pray from. It is not only a trade and exchange from Heaven, but My [Constructive] Trust works and thereby 'empowers, restores, and dismantles' the powers of darkness. It is a bridge to cross over, filling the gap between what the demonic realm created and the portal of My Glory.

Wiktionary.com's definition of a constructive trust is:

> *A trust created by a court (regardless of the intent of the parties) to benefit a party that has been wrongfully deprived of its rights.*[66]

As Joyce was praying for LifeSpring, she heard Father say, "Receive the Trust now for them and for yourselves. Establish the 'Trust of Unity.'"

She prayed:

Father, I request access to the Court of Records to request a constructive trust, a platform established by Heaven according to Psalm 11:3 which says: 'If the foundations be destroyed, what can the righteous do?'

> Then she heard, *"Replace My Word, My Grace, the trust being the foundation of God's Word, a measure of His grace."*

She continued her prayer:

Father, I request the following constructive trusts:

- *Constructive Trust of Unity*
- *Constructive Trust of Racial Harmony & Freedom*
- *Constructive Trust of Brotherhood and Sisterhood in Christ*
- *Constructive Trust of One race, one blood*
- *Constructive Trust for Divine Pathways to be Restored*

---

[66] https://duckduckgo.com/?t=ffab&q=constructive+trust+definition&ia=definition

- Constructive Trust of Harvest Returned for the Body of Christ & LifeSpring International Ministries
- Constructive Trust of Comfort of the Brethren one to another
- Constructive Trust Communion and fellowship in the Holy Spirit, Amen.

I immediately saw the paperwork being prepared.

I asked the Lord where the Trusts were to be established and He said, "Ask Me," so I did. I was led to request constructive trusts for the following:

- *Dr. Ron and staff*
- *Those attached or connected to the LifeSpring International Ministries*
- *The Body of Christ*
- *Those who will listen to LifeSpring.*

I could see a white blanket which reminded me of the dominion Stephanie spoke about.

I receive the constructive trust now, in Jesus' name.

Psalm 37:4 came to mind which says, "Delight yourself also in the LORD, And He shall give you the desires of your heart."

I requested the assistance of the angels of the Trust Department to administer the constructive trust, like a sheet or platform to the realms involved, completely, accurately, securely, and firmly.

I then thanked the Lord for what was received.

As more understanding of the value and need for constructive trusts is unveiled, we shall see lives impacted in fresh and powerful ways.

Many of us have been deprived of our rights. We need legal means to gain those rights back. This is a fresh tool for the Body of Christ to embrace.

———·———

Chapter 16
The Kingdom Dynamics of Being a Living Rainbow

We are outside with a beautiful hilly view, but there are mountains in front of us. In the distance, we are looking at a rainbow.

Envision with us and look at the beauty of this landscape. It is like a landscape painting. Everything has its place. Everything is in its place. In this, we are looking at the promises of God—the inheritance that is for the sons. People can glean from these promises.

Think of the rainbow when you think of the revelation that is coming forth.

Think of the Rainbow

Let it be a reminder—this landscape, this rainbow that as you are walking in this revelation, as it is becoming known, these too, are the promises of God, and are just as evident as the rainbow has been with the understanding of what God did in Genesis. His promises regarding these revelations are just as prominent, just as relevant, just as secure. The Father wants the people to know this and learn about His love abounding through trades.

His love abounds
in His promises to us,
those that know
and assume their sonship
should fully see the rainbow.

The promise is that this revelation is coming from the Throne of God. In that promise, we can rest. This promise is more than just a natural rainbow that people will see. They will see this played out in their lives. Others will see the changes in them—the newness, the peace they will experience in and of themselves—a *living* rainbow of promises. Others can view us as a living rainbow.

The promise of God, instead of it being an actual rainbow in the sky, will be the living, breathing, walking promise of God of this revelation—*us!*

The Living Testament

This freedom, this place of freedom, this place of promise—is for the sons.

> Be the living Testament
> of the rainbow.

Walk in it. We will be amazed at those that are drawn to it. Father wants all His sons to enjoy this place. It is an inheritance that belongs to the sons. Seek it.

Matthew 6:33 says, *"Seek first, the Kingdom of God and all its righteousness, and all these things will be added unto you."*[67] That is what this place is. All these things that are added unto us. This is part of that!

People have been looking for an escape for an exceedingly long time. They find it in other things. They find it in other religions, meditation, and occult practices. They find it in drugs and alcohol. *This* is what they are seeking. This is what the Father offers to the sons. This is a reprieve. This is a place to come. It is a true gift. Take it.

Lydia had just appeared, so she and Stephanie stood quietly admiring the scenery.

Stephanie asked, "Lydia, what questions do I need to ask you about this? Is this a display of Heaven for us to enjoy in the moment?"

She turned and said, "Yes, that is what this place is. This is what the Father wants for His sons—a place of reprieve as they walk in their sonship—as they truly

---

[67] Matthew 6:33

begin to understand who they are. This is what Heaven has to offer as an inheritance for them now. Not when they come here when their bodies die, but it is for them. Now!"

She then showed Stephanie a picture of the world as if she were in outer space, and she was looking at it with the turmoil that is in it.

Stephanie said, "It was like there were two halves of the world and they were shifting back and forth, and the world was in great turmoil."

Lydia said, "The turmoil upon the earth is increasing, and the Father wants a place for His people to be able to land. This is what this is. Walk out your sonship. Walk it out, and be the living testament of the promise. You have full access here."

Stephanie replied, "Lydia, thank you for this. I do know many of us have understood that we can step in, participate, and be in the realms of Heaven. This is where we can find peace. It is where we can come before the Just Judge."

Lydia said, "Yes, but many do not realize that they are the product. As they walk in this, they are a part of it. It is tangible."

Stephanie said to me, "She just showed me people searching for the pot of gold at the end of the rainbow."

Lydia said, "People will seek you out. They will be drawn to you."

Stephanie asked, "Is this related to the Halls of Commerce?"

Lydia replied, "All of this is related."

The Bond of the Promise

Stephanie remarked, "Now we are in that upper conference room, but through the window, I can still see the rainbow. She spoke to Ezekiel, who was present, "Hi Ezekiel! I see a lot of your ranks and commanders. I see my angel Citadel."

Stephanie noted, "He is large again in my presence," and asked, "Ezekiel, do you have something to say?"

He turned towards the window where she could still see the landscape with the rainbow outside the window, and he waved his hand across the window as if showing the panorama.

She said, "Ezekiel, I feel like it is a commissioning."

Ezekiel said, "It is. It is a Bond of The Promise."

She asked, "Ezekiel, are you showing me that this is a Bond of The Promise?"

She said, "I see now it is a bond that we can request of the Father and commission the angels, and the angels can bring to us the promise that allows us to be able to fully comprehend and move in this. The scripture from

Acts, '*in Him we live and move and have our being of being*'[68] came to mind."

Ezekiel said, "That is what this bond will bring."

Stephanie remarked, "He is showing me the landscape and that the Bond of The Promise is like an instruction of ordered steps. It feels like it helps as we commission our angels, to order our steps. This is part of that. It creates more of an ease of being able to walk as a living testament of the promise."

Ezekiel said, "As we release this upon those that do not understand this work, it also allows their spirit to be able to take a hold of this bond and begin to work it out in their lives. They will be drawn to those that walk in it and they will have the ability to walk it out on their own more easily. It creates an ease, but it is a bond."

Stephanie began,

Father, we ask for access into Court of Titles and Deeds, and we request on behalf of LifeSpring Ministries, and all of those that are drawn to it, all those that trade with it, all of those that work for it and their families, we request the release of the Bond of The Promise with a writ of release of ease to the people.

We commission Ezekiel, his commanders, and his ranks, and we commission our angels to go help

---

[68] Acts 17:28

deliver these bonds to the people in the name of Jesus.

Ezekiel just turned to me, and he said, "You have just made a trade." Then he winked and went away.

Stephanie commented, "This is why Heaven knows that the people need to hear this. I just saw a picture of me in prayer, where there are days that it feels hard or you are going through something, to be able to step into this place, however people see, hear, or sense and see the rainbow and then take it upon themselves to be that. Then ease comes as a reminder of all the promises that are here."

Wisdom, Knowledge, and Understanding were also present in the room and Stephanie said, "Hi, Wisdom. Thank you for being here."

Wisdom replied, "This is the wisdom of God to impart peace amid turmoil. It is a reminder of His promises where many have lost hope. Many in the body have lost much hope. Father is in the reminding business. It is just a reminder. It is a reminder to the people of His promise. This place is His promise that we can be walking versions of that. This is just a reminder of that promise."

Stephanie replied, "Thank you. Wisdom, Knowledge, and Understanding. I can see Ezekiel way in the distance, and I see the angels bringing this bond to people."

Chapter 17
The Kingdom Dynamics of Co-Laboring

As we engaged Heaven again, the room was suddenly filled with Angels. Ezekiel appeared and we asked, "Is there a commissioning that you need?"

We heard a commissioning so, Stephanie began,

> *I commission you, your ranks, and your commanders to break the standard of old. To remove its powers, its frequencies, its hindrances, its telecommunications, its systems. Do this by use of every Capturing Bag, in time and out of time and in every dimension and take it and destroy it, in the name of Jesus. Use the armaments of Heaven and the weaponry of Heaven. Use your good skill, in Jesus' name.*
>
> *I commission you to take the banner and replace the old banner with the Banner of the Lord—to stake it, mark it, and highlight it, in Jesus' name!*

The angels were all still standing with us so apparently, we were not finished. Stephanie continued,

Father, I ask on all their behalf, angel food, bread, and elixir.

She noted, "Now they're leaving."

The lights in the room we were in dimmed and a movie began playing on the screen that had appeared. Everyone in the room was watching a movie of some angelic activity. One could see a variety of landscapes. Some with cities and towns. One could see a mapping of people's minds. Scattered about the landscape the angels were planting red flags (banners) where the territories had been reclaimed and restored. The flags were on tall poles so the enemy could see that this was territory that had been taken and given back to the Kingdom of Heaven because of the blood of Jesus, because of the commissioning, because of the co-laboring, because of the obedience. The movie explained that this is the reason this movement is taking place.

Stephanie commented, "Lydia and Malcolm, when you say movement, there's a double meaning. I see the movement of when the earth moves under the force of an earthquake as it realigns itself and shifts and I see a movement, as in the body, coming together and moving in unison. Its march step is in unison. When they stake these banners in the ground, initially the ground is barren. Then, it turns lush after the banner is staked in the ground. There is an enumerable number of angels doing this work. That is why it was so crowded in the room. They were pressed up almost against me.

"Malcolm said, 'Taste and see that the Lord is good.'"[69] Stephanie continued, "I'm watching Malcom and Lydia be in awe, wonder, and joy of what this movie is showing."

She asked, "Is this a result of the new revelation or of the Kingdom Dynamics of Heaven and all that we have learned?"

Malcom said "It is because we chose the Kingdom of Heaven. We choose the co-laboring. We chose the partnership. We chose the love of our Savior and of our Father. This is a direct result of all those things. This is Kingdom Dynamics."

We chose:

- the Kingdom of Heaven
- the co-laboring with angels & men & women in white
- the partnership with Heaven
- the love of our Savior and of our Father.

Stephanie said, "Dr. Ron, I'm seeing land and I'm also seeing people's minds that were barren and ugly, like scorched earth becoming lush green with a deep colored color. Angels are really planting these banners high. What is significant is that I don't view it or see it as we

---

[69] Psalm 34:8

would see these banners. It is like how they used to capture kingdoms and they would put the new flag up. That's what this is—capturing of dominions and domains. Overturning the principalities is exactly that. It's putting up the new flag. Thank you, Father."

The movie ended and they turned the lights back on in the room.

Wisdom came in and said, "I'm pleased with the revelation that's been revealed and is being utilized—because of the importance of it, because we are dealing with principalities." She reiterated to us the importance of us utilizing her in every scenario and situation when it comes to that work. She gave Stephanie a big pearl much larger than one she had been given on a prior engagement. With that, Wisdom went and stood along the wall.

Jesus was also in the room now and the room was filled with His love. It enveloped the room. He said, "Because the people have been freed of the domination of the dominion, they will begin to experience My love. They will begin to experience the relational freedom that people will find in this as the banners are being raised and the flags are being turned back to Me. As the territories are returned to Me, these stakes are placed in the ground."

———·———

Chapter 18
The Kingdom Dynamics of Governing Our Territory

The sound we could hear resonating over the sound of the waterfall we were near was the question, "Are you ready to put your soul down?" The voice came from someone we had never engaged with before—John the Baptist. We were honored to meet him, but he downplayed the event saying "I'm honored because *you* are here. You are just as much **sons** as I am."

When asked what he wanted to speak with us about, he simply said, "I want to show you grace."

We then followed him and stepped *through* the waterfall. We walked through a very short cavern and out to the other side. We came to a landscape where he began to explain some things to us.

There is grace in governing. John governed the wilderness. It didn't govern him. He understood the grace he carried to govern. At first, it was compounded by fear, but when he realized the grace that he was *in at the time* and in what was coming, he was able to govern *in* the grace. Grace isn't just a word you throw around and say, "Oh, I give you grace." Grace isn't just a word.

---

*Grace is a governing authority,
a governance, a stance,
and from that place,
our authority rises.
We become.*

The landscape and the footing for the sons are right in front of them. Choosing grace to govern from *is* a first step. This *is* dimensional.

Laying down of flesh is a part of governing by grace. We have thrown around the word grace to people our whole lives and never used it in a position of authority to walk in and to govern our own landscape and territory, but this was the beginning of the imagination of our territories.

We were in a dimensional place that John governed from. It was his territory that he governed from. Its expanse was wide. It reached far but where do we think he received the grace to govern from? *He accepted the journey.*

We noticed that John had writing on the soles of his feet, and he exclaimed, *"The steps of a righteous man are ordered of the Lord.*"[70] Even here he laid his flesh down on earth and this was his reward. John was part of teaching us how we were going to begin to understand as sons that we will be able to govern in other realms and other dimensions in quantum.

We followed John and where we were standing, we could see a huge landscape. But when we took a few more steps the entire landscape changed—as if we had walked into another time. In fact, we did.

We stepped from one place to another—in time, out of time, ahead of time, behind time, there is no time in Heaven.

The grace in governing is the assurance of your steps.

They are assured here by the Father Himself.

The grace that John had, is to step in these places.

Grace is Also a Condition

There are conditions in governance. This walk is *by faith* **through grace.**

While we had been talking, John turned, and we went where he had gone, back through the cavern. We came to the other side, through the waterfall, back where we

---

[70] Psalm 37:23

started. We could see his feet. He was standing here in front of us with one foot on a rock. One foot was a little elevated on another rock or boulder, and his feet were vibrating. The rest of him was not, but his feet were. It was a sound, a vibration, and a frequency.

Territories & Landscapes

Our territory is our made up of our realms. We are a territory, and our territory has realms. Territories consist of realms and realms make up territories. For example, LifeSpring is a territory. It has many realms. Our families are territories that are made of various realms. They all make up the territory that we get to govern.

These territories are in time, out of time, ahead of time, and there is no time in Heaven. This quantum leaping into other paradigms is part of the governance of our own territories.

We realized that although Heaven had taught us about dominions and realms, they had not taught us much about territories. They have always talked about dominions. We wanted some clarity on territories, so we asked Malcolm if he could assist us.

Malcolm inquired, "How did you like that?"

Stephanie replied, "I liked it! Malcolm, that was a true gift from the Father."

Malcolm replied, "Yes. That's the stance in Heaven as sons. You're a son, Ron's a son, John's a son. This isn't celebrity status we are talking about here."

We are *all on an equal plane* as sons. This goes to the verse about, "*God is no respecter of persons.*"[71]

Governance is a different platform in these dimensions than it is on earth, but they carry some of the same flavor.

---

*Governance here is at **and** by the hand of the Father. Governance on earth is a ruling order.*

Do we have a grace to govern our own realm?

The only grace that we have is *through* the Father, through Jesus, to ourselves. It is never *in **and** of* ourselves, even the governing of our own territory. This is where the rubber meets the road. Dying to ourselves has a whole new meaning.

We may have heard it our whole lives, about dying to ourselves but not grasping what that truly means. There have probably been just a few that really understood that. We were here, wanting to understand territory vs. landscape.

---

[71] Acts 10:34

Describing what she was seeing, Stephanie said, "All of a sudden, we are walking. A stream is on my left. There is just open land, trees, and grass.

Malcolm asked, "What would you call this?"

Stephanie replied, "Malcolm, I would call it a landscape."

Malcolm responded, "Is it? Or is it a territory?"

Stephanie remarked, "I don't know. Malcolm. You're going to have to define it for me."

Malcolm explained that a territory is something we own—we own it because it's a part of us. A landscape is a time. A landscape is the time and effort put in *as* sons to *develop* the territory—to envelope a territory.

Next Malcolm showed us a vacant territory. The landscape was "without form. It was void." As we walk in our landscape, it is developed over time. Landscape is also *a result of trade.* Look at the dominion and domain work of the enemy. When we trade from it, it creates its own landscape versus how we trade in things of righteousness through grace. Trading in righteousness creates a landscape that is pristine and beautiful. When we walk on landscapes, we can have stumbling blocks when someone has traded from hell.

Cleaning up of the generations is not a reset of the landscape, but it's a clearing off the landscape. The value in generational work is that the Father, through His grace and on our behalf, pulls the stumbling blocks off, brings in the other Godly trades from Heaven, and then the landscape changes. It's why our steps matter.

How we walk spiritually matters, because it creates the landscape in front of us. Consider our next step. What is it going to look like? Have we created stumbling blocks for ourselves with what we have traded with? That's why we spoke about the golden path.[72]

Territory is a dominion matter.
Landscape is a heart matter.

Landscape is *what* we have sown, and it is what is reaped.

When Malcolm said the word 'sow,' we saw it as, when we sow in righteousness on fertile ground, we saw an instantaneous time lapse, first of fertile ground, seed, and growth. We could see on other side of that, across the road, when we sow in bitterness and hatred and all those other sins, the landscape is very scorched.

This is where Hosea 10:12 comes in.

Sow for yourselves righteousness; reap in mercy; break up your fallow ground, for it is time to seek the LORD, till He comes and rains righteousness on you.

---

[72] Described in the blog post on "The Golden Pathway" on CourtsOfHeavenWebinars.com

We are sowing to *create* a landscape.

As we meditated on this engagement, we realized that the first example in scripture of governing a territory and fashioning a landscape occurred in Genesis 1 where the Scripture points out in Genesis 1:2-19:

> *The earth was without form, and void; and darkness was on the face of the deep. And the Spirit of God was hovering over the face of the waters. ³ Then God said, "Let there be light"; and there was light. ⁴ And God saw the light, that it was good; and God divided the light from the darkness. ⁵ God called the light Day, and the darkness He called Night. So, the evening and the morning were the first day.*

God began governing the formless planet known as Earth and the first thing He did was release light upon it. Where did the light come from? It makes no mention of the creation of suns or stars, yet. I surmise that it was the Glory of God that illuminated the planet at that point.

> *⁶ Then God said, "Let there be a firmament in the midst of the waters, and let it divide the waters from the waters." ⁷ Thus God made the firmament, and divided the waters which were under the firmament from the waters which were above the firmament; and it was so. ⁸ And God called the firmament Heaven. So, the evening and the morning were the second day.*

The next day He divided the waters from the firmament and dry land appeared. God had just begun developing the landscape. He then called forth vegetation onto the planet.

> [9] Then God said, "Let the waters under the heavens be gathered together into one place, and let the dry land appear"; and it was so. [10] And God called the dry land Earth, and the gathering together of the waters He called Seas. And God saw that it was good. [11] Then God said, "Let the earth bring forth grass, the herb that yields seed, and the fruit tree that yields fruit according to its kind, whose seed is in itself, on the earth"; and it was so. [12] And the earth brought forth grass, the herb that yields seed according to its kind, and the tree that yields fruit, whose seed is in itself according to its kind. And God saw that it was good. [13] So the evening and the morning were the third day.

God was quite busy on the third day, but on the fourth day he began to landscape the heavens. He instituted these things so that mankind, who was to come later, would have daily rest cycles and to provide natural light to the inhabitants of the planet.

> [14] Then God said, "Let there be lights in the firmament of the heavens to divide the day from the night; and let them be for signs and seasons, and for days and years; [15] and let them be for lights in the firmament of the heavens to give light

> on the earth"; and it was so. ¹⁶ Then God made two great lights: the greater light to rule the day, and the lesser light to rule the night. **He made the stars also.** ¹⁷ God set them in the firmament of the heavens to give light on the earth, ¹⁸ and to rule over the day and over the night, and to divide the light from the darkness. And God saw that it was good. ¹⁹ So the evening and the morning were the fourth day. (Emphasis added)

God not only created the sun, but also the moon as a light reflective surface to provide light during nighttime hours. He made stars also (v. 16) and set them in the heavens to give light (direction/illumination) to the earth. Psalm 119 tells us that God's Word is a lamp unto our feet and a light unto our path. His Word is not just transcribed into the Bible, but also in the scrolls of destiny that pertain to each of us. These words also provide illumination and direction. Notice that he says the stars give light/illumination/direction to the earth and they also rule over the day and the night. This will be significant to us as we will see in the chapter about Moses. The illumination of stars divides light (direction) from darkness (wandering).

It is interesting that Genesis 1 speaks of stars governing the day and night. We don't think of stars as governing—and that is distinct from the sun and moon who rule. However, the word translated stars in that verse has a figurative meaning of a prince—a ruler.

In the governing from Heaven, which is what we are doing when we govern from our star, notice that God placed lights in the sky and stars, also. What are the lights in the sky if not the stars? What are the stars apart from the lights?

Those are questions to inquire of the Lord concerning. Job would be a good place to begin looking.

> ¹ Then the LORD answered Job out of the whirlwind, and said:
>
> ⁷ (Where were you) when **the morning stars sang together, And all the sons of God shouted for joy?** ⁸ "Or who shut in the sea with doors, When it burst forth and issued from the womb; ⁹ When I made the clouds its garment, And thick darkness its swaddling band; ¹⁰ When I fixed My limit for it, And set bars and doors; ¹¹ When I said, 'This far you may come, but no farther, And here your proud waves must stop!' ¹² Have you **commanded the morning** since your days began, And **caused the dawn to know its place**, ¹³ That it might take hold of the ends of the earth, And the wicked be shaken out of it? ¹⁴ It takes on form like clay under a seal, And stands out like a garment. (Job 38:7-14) (Emphasis added)

Other scriptures talk about this subject which is one to inquire of Heaven about. More insights will be unveiled later in this book.

Chapter 19
The Kingdom Dynamics of Agreement

When we engaged Heaven this day and approached the Help Desk, we found Lydia behind the desk.

She announced, "There is great preparation in the Kingdom right now. There is a great momentum forward. The momentum forward is established in Kingdom Principles—Kingdom Dynamics and weighty aspects of time. We are in a *time* and a *season*, and we are in a *season* and a *time*. The season and a time are the growth. This is a growing season, and it is for such a time as this.

"The great revelatory work is in this season and time and in this time and season. Our focus can be on the ordained manifestations, processes, ideas, ideals, and work. It is seasoned."

Stephanie was instructed to climb a large clock-tower she had seen. From the vantage point at the top of it, she could see angels in warfare. She was seeing the spiritual realm of where angels and fallen angels fight. She was also hearing trumpets—victory trumpets.

While this massive amount of angelic warfare was going on, she could sense the victory. She was hearing the victory sounds. It was as if she had peeked over a realm and was looking into a different realm.

The fighting suddenly ended. In the way that it ended, two things happened. First, it was as if the sun rose immediately. It was a giant sun, but we knew it was the Son of God—the light that came up. Things looked gray initially (in the original picture) while she was looking at it. It was very gray and not bright at all. The sun came up and there was light penetrating. There was a clap of thunder, then everything stopped. The fallen angels were defeated. Cleanup work began being done by the angels. Angels were picking up carcasses.

What we were seeing represented the defeat of the decay of flesh. As the spirit rises, there is a conquering voice, manner, speech, sound, and light that will be felt that will dismantle the kingdom of darkness. It is what it looks like in the spirit when the flesh has been defeated to advance forward. This is what John the Baptist did. He, on earth, had the grace to reign in that realm. He laid his flesh down. It was how he was able to move in that paradigm. It was how Jesus was able to be in two places at the same time.

Lydia had shown us the spiritual aspect of what that means when Heaven told us recently about laying down our flesh to move in this next step. That is what this was. It felt like the appearance of the sun was the awakening of the sons to their sonship. The clap of thunder was the agreement between the Father's voice and the son's voices that put a halt to where we, as sons, are trying to do dimensional and paradoxical things. It is as if, in the second heaven, that obstruction was defeated.

As we learn who we are as sons, it is an agreement—an agreement of being a son with the agreement of the Father's voice about us being sons.

It is something that seems to contradict itself, but which is nevertheless true.

Stephanie climbed down from the big, tall clock tower and remarked how her feet never felt like they weren't on solid ground. It felt completely solid and safe. It represented the solid ground of the paradox and the paradigm we were learning about which are based on the principles and foundations *of* the Most High.

Just like this ministry is in a new position and a new positioning, Lydia informed us that she grows with it. These are the next steps, and we have gone up higher. We have gone to the next level.

As we returned to the Help Desk, no one was present but a tent card that said, "The dawning of a new Day.

The Instruction

Stephanie picked up the card and read, "*An instruction regarding obstruction.*"

I spoke to Stephanie and said, "Let me give you a thought about that. See the sign. Place it in front of you as if it were going to grow to be 10' by 10' sign and *step into* what it says."

Stephanie replied, "Okay. I can do that." She took a step into the words on the card and found herself standing on the word 'obstruction.'

I remarked, "Now ask, 'What do you have to teach us about this today?'"

The page began to instruct us saying light overcomes the darkness, as we all know. *Instruction* overcomes *obstruction*. This is quantum. Instruction wields like a sword. Think of it as titanium-strength body-blows to what obstruction would bring.

Stephanie said, "When I heard, 'what obstruction would bring,' it was more of a feeling of something being obstructed and as the sword went through it and cut it, it dismantled the word and the feeling of obstruction."

Instruction illuminates. Instruction cast its eyes down upon obstruction as if it were looking down on it. The way we would view someone looking down upon someone else. That is what this is. It is putting obstruction in its place. Instruction puts obstruction in its place and dismantles it.

Instruction not only illuminates, but it also cauterizes the bleeding. Think of it as a vessel being filled where an obstruction has come in and pierced the vessel and there is a bleeding out of what has been placed in that vessel, like truth and light and the Word. Instruction cauterizes those open places that were obstructed—where men's minds have been obstructed, men's hearts have been obstructed, men's views have been obstructed.

What *IS* the instruction?

Authority is an instruction. Forgiveness is an instruction. Usurping[73] is an instruction. Religious dismantling is an instruction.

The traction of trust is an instruction.

Trust gives us a sure footing about an arena. Leveraging the word is an instruction. Defining the components is an instruction. And above all things—*love* is an instruction.

Let's go down a rabbit hole about 'above all—love.' It took me a couple of places. It was the laying down of my

---

[73] As in usurping the working of the enemy, as demonstrated when Jesus overthrew the tables of the moneychangers in the temple.

life for another. That does not mean death in the physical. It means laying down of our abilities, our time, our generosity, on behalf of another. It is what we do in the paradigm of the time that we spend on behalf of others in the Courts of Heaven. That is a laying down. It also is a laying down of flesh, of what our carnal nature would want to do, considering what we just went through (with a team member) and what that looks like. That was the second rabbit hole. We laid down pieces of our flesh to love through that. It cannot be any other way. There is no room for that as we walk in this way of being. There is no room for the flesh at all. Heaven keeps saying it must be laid down completely.

Offense is an error. Our recent experience was an example.[74] It felt like a dying of our flesh when we do not rear our own head up in offense.

I now have felt that Heaven has truly understood when we have been hurt and wounded in an offense, but they also know so clearly the reality that there is no place for offense to move forward in quantum with offense. Offense is an obstruction to keep us from going into that next. We must die to ourselves. We *cannot* be in offense. We must forgive. All of it is totally coming together in this—the Courts of Heaven and all the Courts of Heaven represents is forgiveness and repentance. There is no

---

[74] We had a recent situation where someone became deeply offended with me, and we had to choose to have no retaliatory offense in return.

other way to move forward in quantum without continually doing that and living that.

These words are our footing in standing on these words. When there is movement about us, we will not ever feel it because of the surefootedness of standing on these instructions. There could be an earthquake underneath our feet of everything going on around us, and we would never feel it.

Love is the door. Taking on Christ's love as a garment is the surefootedness in which we will stand. Love is the means in which we will be able to walk in the laying down of our flesh. Perfect love casts out fear and *the only reason* the flesh raises its ugly head is *because of fear*. The instruction of perfect love is we do not think that, as sons, we cannot walk in this perfect love as mere men. As mere men we cannot, but as sons we can. These are the instructions.

The Battering Ram

Changing subjects, Stephanie said, "Ezekiel, we call you near and your commanders and ranks." He appeared with his Commander and with a battering ram flung over his left shoulder.

I asked, "Do we need a commission for that?"

Stephanie commented, "The commander has paperwork in his hand, and said the word, 'Strategies.'"

Stephanie began a commissioning,

Ezekiel, we commission you, your commanders, and ranks on behalf of LifeSpring Ministries, its employees, its families, and those that trade with it:

Use the battering ram toward the obstructions, and on the obstructions. As we have said yes to the instructions of Heaven, take the strategies, and the capture bags and lay them upon the time wheels.

Order the steps and lay the foundation before us, ahead of time, in time and out of time, in every dimension—quantumly on the grid.

Use the force of the battering ram and plunder the kingdom of darkness.

Use the green bags, plunder the kingdom of darkness, and bring back to the Kingdom of Heaven, to LifeSpring, its employees, its team members, for the storehouses, in Jesus' name.

Stephanie said, "I was contemplating why I was still seeing him standing there when he said he had already come and gone."

Ezekiel replied, "We had already gone and come back—quantumly."

Stephanie remarked, "And the fighting I saw earlier had already been done quantumly before I even said the words of that commissioning. There is no time in the spirit. Thank you, Ezekiel, for the cleanup work that you and your angels have been doing, because you already did it, didn't you?"

Ezekiel said to Stephanie, "You're getting it."

Stephanie replied, "Am I? Yes, I am."

She prayed,

Father, we commend these angels, all of them that are assigned to LifeSpring Ministries, their commanders, ranks, and patrols—all of them. We call our angels, those that are assigned to every aspect of the ministry, and those that are assigned to our employees, and their families, and those that trade with us.

We commend them all to you and Father, we ask for angel food, bread, and elixir for them.

Thank you, Father for this understanding and knowledge of the greater things of the Kingdom of Heaven. Thank You that You have seen us worthy of this,

Father, we say yes to You and every aspect of what You are doing.

Stephanie remarked, "It is the coolest thing ever to walk on these words like we are walking on a carpet of words."

I commented, "Because it is quantum, we can step into it. We could step into the beginning of that word, and it would be different than what is at the end of that word.

Stephanie said, "I know. We had stepped into the vision of the war that had already happened before the commission was even done!"

I added, "So when we couple that with the amendment of 'As if it never were...'"

Stephanie said, "Oh wow. It has all new meaning."

I remarked,

Quantum is simply finding out what the Bible has already said.

Chapter 20
The Kingdom Dynamics of Knowing Our Star

When we engaged Heaven this time, we had no idea the revelation Heaven was about to unveil to us. Now would be a good time to remind our soul to stay in rest mode with our spirit forward as we read this chapter.

As we engaged Heaven, Stephanie could hear the song, "There is a Fountain." The path we were on was one we had seen before with landscape around us. The path curved around a lovely landscape, and one could hear water from a bubbling brook and a waterfall in the distance. As we meandered along the pathway, we came into view of the waterfall. It was much bigger than the one we had seen when we were with John the Baptist. Stephanie could feel the mist of the water and asked, "What are we doing here?"

Ezekiel appeared with a very large sword and stuck it in the pool of water that was in front of the waterfall.

He turned the sword like we would turn a key. As he did, the waterfall split open, and he instructed us to go in.

Stephanie asked, "Ezekiel, is this a place you go with us?"

He replied, "No, I'm just opening the portal."

Stephanie remarked, "Thank you, Ezekiel, for opening the portal the way you did. I am getting ready to go through the waterfall."

As we stepped through, she commented on how she could smell the dampness. She saw a light at the end of the tunnel we were passing through.

As we stepped through, it was hard to see anything due to the brightness. Adjusting her sight to the surroundings, she realized we were in a beautiful forest. We could see very tall trees, and I could hear water here, too.

She remarked, "I am so interested right now to know where we are. I know we are in a different dimension. Somebody is speaking to me. When I said, 'I know we're in a different dimension,' they said,

'You're actually in a different time.'"

The person said, "*Think prism.*"

Stephanie asked me, "What's a gyroscope?"

I replied, "It is a wheel within a wheel."

The person said, "Think gyroscope."

Stephanie explained, "We can go in every direction. I still do not know who is talking to me, but it is like a voice coming from everywhere. Whoever this is said, 'Take a step forward,' so, I took a step forward and that voice said, 'Turn and take a step backwards.'"

As Stephanie did, she realized that whatever step she took, forward, backward, or sideways, the scenery would change.

She described what she was seeing, "With one step it changed to a scene of an ocean. I am up on a rock, and I am looking down at the ocean. It is beautiful. But when I take a step back, I am back in the forest. I am going to turn, and I am going to take a step backwards."

I explained, "We are looking in different places every time."

Stephanie exclaimed, "Yes!"

I suggested, "Take a step."

As she did, Stephanie said, "When I took a step back, I am in the cleft of the rocks that I've been in before."

I said, "Take a look to your left, now look to the right. You will see different things."

Stephanie remarked, "On my right, I am seeing this garden and a wall of ivy and flowers. As I turn to the left, I see a wall of stone, but it is pretty."

I recommended, "Right now. Look up, look a little more behind you like you are looking just above your books, on the bookshelf in your office."

Stephanie replied, "Okay."

As she looked in that direction she remarked, "There's the waterfall."

I said, "Now you can actually go in-between, you can see both."

Stephanie asked, "What do you mean?"

I instructed, "If you turn your head to the right slowly, you may actually be able to see both at the same time."

Stephanie said, "I can see the waterfall *and* the stone wall now. Yes. I am dimensional, I am seeing this one way back, and one closer. I am going to take a chance to look down."

I said, "Okay. Go ahead, but do it slowly."

Stephanie replied, "I will. I am standing on—well, what looks like the top of a universe, just looking down. I see stars, and I see rings."

I remarked, "It is like you are on one of those Chinese bridges with a glass bottom. Now, stand to your feet and do this. It will be easier for you."

She stood to her feet and exclaimed, "Oh, wow!"

I instructed her, "Now when you look down, rotate to your right"

Stephanie said, "I can see different doorways or dimensions. The triangle that came down and then the triangle that went up this way after the next one.[75] Is it different paradigms or dimensions?" She suddenly noticed a giant star next to where she was. She said, "I can put my hand on it. Wow!"

I said to Stephanie, "Well, introduce yourself."

Stephanie said, "Hi, I am Stephanie. Nice to meet you."

I asked Stephanie, "Did it speak to you or just give you a knowing?"

Stephanie said, "He gave me a knowing, and I've only heard this other person ever speak one time. But he said Ian Clayton's name and asked me if I knew Ian, and I don't."

Stephanie continued, "He (the star) is telling me that I have been to this, I am at the place that Ian has visited. Yes. I am so excited right now. Nice to meet you. I want to come back again."

The star replied, "Oh, you will."

Stephanie said, "Okay. I have not looked up yet."

I replied, "Don't do that yet, but as you are looking down and as you rotate, the scenery shifts again. Do it slowly."

Stephanie commented, "I can see levels now. On one side are levels."

---

[75] Described in the blog post on "The Golden Pathway."

I replied, "They are below you, above you, beneath you, and to your sides.

Stephanie noted, "They *are* around me. They are everywhere. We are on a level and there are levels below us and above us. Are these levels of Heaven?

I replied, "Not necessarily."

Stephanie said, "I felt a breeze. Like a shift. It is a movement, and I felt the breeze of that."

I mentioned, "Now you are in a different place than you were just a moment ago."

Stephanie remarked, "I am going to step towards this waterfall. Now, it is right in front of me, and I am going to step back. I'm going to step towards this wall that I see that is so beautiful. It has moss in between each stone. This is an ancient place. My mind is officially ecstatic and blown at the same time. It is the coolest thing ever. Oh, somebody just said 'Not ever.' Okay. I come out of agreement with myself saying that is the coolest thing ever, because apparently, there's more. Thank you for showing us this."

The voice said, "It's a dimensional walk."

Stephanie observed, "I am standing in this very large forest. There are a lot of trees, but there's also a lot of room in between the trees, and they are very tall. There isn't brush at the bottom or anything like that. It is just trees. I do see someone. The bright light in this forest is massive. In the distance, I see someone's shadow.

I suggested, "Step toward them." As she did, she was immediately where she was going.

Stephanie said, "I stepped toward the shadow of the person and the scenery changed to the ocean. I am standing on this cliff by the ocean, and I see that person down by the ocean on the sand. I am going take another step, and instantly, I am in front of them. Their back is to me. I can tell that they have rugged features from the back, but they have not turned around. They have kind of long hair, and it reminds me of the clothing in the Moses movie with Charleston Heston. That is what the back looks like. It reminds me of that. He still has not turned around. I can hear the water lapping up on the shore where I am standing. I can feel the sand. He just spoke and said, 'It's not sinking sand.'

"No, it is not," Stephanie replied.

He then said, "Are you ready for me to turn around?"

She replied, "I am."

He said, "Are you sure?"

She answered again, "I am. I am sure."

As she said that, he turned, and she instantly knew it was Moses because the scripture came to her about how his face shone with the Glory of the Lord. His face was still shining.

She greeted him saying, "Moses, it is very nice to meet you. I am honored."

Moses said, "Take your time, Stephanie. Take it in."

Stephanie remarked, "I am just looking at his features. He is a rather burly man. He is big in the shoulders, and he does have a beard. I keep seeing this red cover, like a sash on him and it is alive."

Moses remarked, "It's the first thing Jesus place around me when I stepped into Heaven."

Stephanie noted, "It is alive. It moves. It has a movement to it. It is significant."

To Moses, she said, "I do not understand why you are making this really clear to me about the sash that Jesus gave you."

Moses replied, "It belongs to those of us who are of the firstborn."

Stephanie remarked, "That means the firstborn of the church? Can you clarify that for me?"

Moses said, "Jesus was there before He was there."

Stephanie said, "I understood that he meant *there* before there was a *there* on the earth."

Moses explained, "He covered me in this. I was pre-covered. He gave it to those are the firstborn."

Stephanie commented, "You are being a trailblazer, being the firstborn—those of you that stepped into Heaven (like we do now) before we understood what that term meant. That is what you are talking about, isn't it?"

Moses replied, "Walk with me."

Stephanie asked, "This is your territory, isn't it? This is where you rule from?"

Moses replied, "This is a piece of my territory. There are landscapes I walk upon. There are territories I rule from, and there are planes I govern."

Stephanie commented, "We are getting to experience this one? No, we are *walking* upon this one, and we *experienced* early on the other places like the ancient brick wall. He stands at the top of this. He stands at the place where I saw the galaxy underneath—which is where he treads. He treads upon that area and governs."

I replied, "So that's his territory."

Stephanie remarked, "Amazing! and that star—it is as if he and a star put out decrees or rulings."

She continued, "Moses, I am grateful and thankful and privileged that we've been able to see your territory and your landscapes. I know it is the tip of the iceberg, because I just heard you say it."

"He just reminded me of when I read your book, *Engaging the Courts for Your City*[76] and read *Treasures of Darkness*,[77] that I actually said in my spirit that I wanted to trade with Moses, and that's what we're doing right now!"

---

[76] *Engaging the Courts for Your City* by Dr. Ron M. Horner, LifeSpring Publishing (2019).

[77] *Treasures of Darkness, Volume 2: Echoes of the Father* by Joseph C. Sturgeon II, Seraph Creative (2016).

Moses remarked, "This *time* is a trade."

Stephanie replied, "Thank you. I accept this trade, and I give it back. I want to learn more."

Moses asked, "Would you like to go back to that star?"

Stephanie exclaimed, "Yes, take us!"

Describing what she was seeing, Stephanie said, "I have turned and now I see the star, here in front of me. I am watching him with a scroll in hand speaking to the star. He is speaking to the star from the scroll. *It is causing the star to be enlarged.* Not to grow bigger, but it is being enlarged somehow—enhanced.

"Moses, thank you for bringing to me that picture of you, speaking from a scroll to the star and it being enlarged. Could you help me understand the purpose of what that enlargement does for the Kingdom of Heaven?"

Moses said, "Everything the Father has us speak from the scrolls, enlarges the Kingdom."

I asked, "How would *we* do that?"

Moses replied, "Time encapsulates these measures. Agree to the understanding. Co-labor. Gather the scrolls and your destiny. Organize."

Stephanie remarked, "When he said 'organize,' I see the complete co-laboring and working with the angels that would bring the scrolls. It is a *daily* thing."

"Moses, can I simply say to the angels to bring me that scroll for the day and encapsulate the time, reading that scroll?" she asked.

"He then gave me the picture of him doing it," she commented.

Moses said, "This is laying our flesh down, which is our soul, not out of our own heads. This is co-laboring with the angels, asking for the scroll for the day, stepping in, being in agreement with whatever framework Heaven has for the destiny of the day, *through* time, trusting the sound of the words you hear."

Stephanie remarked, "The trusting of the sound—the way he showed me that was we would hear the words and then turn and speak to them. Right, Moses?"

He said, "You have the scroll and as a prophetic act, you can open it up, hear the sound because the angels are co-laboring with you, and they have given you the scroll for the day. Hear the sound, and then speak it.

I asked, "Can we practice that?"

"Stephanie," he said, "know the star."

Moses said, "In our own territories and landscapes, are stars."

Stephanie explained, "Moses just showed me this massive network of people that begin to understand this working together by way of reading the scrolls, working with the encapsulation of time, and that as more people in this earthly realm understand this knowledge and do it, it is enlarging the Kingdom and bringing "Thy Kingdom come, Thy will be done."

Engaging Our Star

I asked, "So how are we introduced to our star?"

Moses replied simply, "Ask for it."

I asked, "Does the ministry have its own star?"

Moses responded, "The ministry has three stars, and you have your own star."

Stephanie discovered she has two stars.

I asked, "Can you walk with us on this Moses?"

Moses replied, "Step one."

I remarked, "Step one is, 'Request to know your star,' right? I request to know my personal star and the three ministry stars."

Stephanie said, "I am looking at you, Ron, standing just above your star as you are about this big in space (making a tiny gesture), and I am looking at your personal star. It is to your left, and I see three more stars. The one to your left wants you to stand on it. It is like you are three inches above it. There is the sense of a rush of air like you have from the back of a jet engine of an airplane when it is about to take off.

"Also, I see those kingly/priestly robes that I saw a few days ago. They are around you. I see you, but around you are all these things—this clothing, the priestly garments, I see the staff you rule with and your signet rings, and I see what looks like a podium and a very large book on it. This is where you speak from."

She then asked, "Moses, is this where he receives scrolls?"

Moses replied, "This is where you come to *read* from your books. From this place, ask the angels to bring you one scroll for the day for the first star, one scroll for the day for the second star, and one scroll for the day for the third star. Each star has a scroll. The book that you are reading from initially is for your own star. You are to ask for the scroll for that star."

I immediately responded, "I ask for the scroll for my personal star today."

Stephanie said, "I see it. An angel is handing it to you. Put it in your heart and you will receive a download."

Moses instructed me, "Commit the star to be the Lord's and the Lord's only."

I replied, "I commit the star to be the Lord's, and the Lord's only."

Moses continued, "It's a territory. Deed it."

I responded, "I surrender the deed of this star to the Lord of Hosts."

Moses said, "Now, call for the scroll of the first ministry star."

Obediently, I said, "I call for the scroll of the first ministry star."

Stephanie remarked, "It is as if you have the force of that jet engine airplane wind under your feet and you have moved above your first star and there is an angel bringing you the scroll and handing it to you. The scroll is very large. It has golden handles on each end. It is also quite thick. You are to stand on it."

Stephanie continued, "When you stood on it, it became what looked like a hoverboard. You are hovering on all points around this star. Do the same thing, commit it to the Lord."

I replied, "I commit this star to the Lord and to be the Lord's only, and I deed the territory of this star to the Lord of hosts."

Stephanie noted, "What's interesting is you are in your priestly garments doing this."

I continued, "I request the scroll for the second star for this day."

Stephanie remarked, "It is a lightning bolt and there are words all over it. It is a staff. You can take that lightning bolt as a staff. The hoverboard you were on with the first star has stayed behind because it was for the first star, but you have gone on to this second star. You are taking the lightning bolt, and you are staking the star in the ground as if to awaken it. When you stake it in the ground, commit it to the Lord and deed it to Him."

I responded, "I commit this star and this scroll to the Lord, and I deed the territory of it to the Lord of host."

Stephanie explained, "When you stuck that lightning bolt into the ground like a stake and made that proclamation, it is like lightning bolts trickled out and went through the star. It went all through it internally. That second star seems to be red in nature, and it has this white lightning bolt going through it. The star is kind of a reddish-brown color. All the lightning bolts have gone through this star.

"Your star to the left is multiple colors of every color purple that is imaginable. The second star is reddish brown in color, but now it has different places where that white is from the lightning bolt went through.

"Now we are back in front of the third star. Call for the scroll."

Immediately, I said, "I call for this scroll of this third star for the day, in Jesus' name."

Stephanie commented, "I am seeing an angel. He just presented the scroll as a red carpet,[78] but it is not red, it is green. As he had presented it in a roll on the ground and walked, he kicked it out and it rolled out, more and more, in front of you. It is green in color and has what looks like short blades of grass, but each blade is a word. Each blade has a word, not in English because this one

---

[78] Like the expression, "roll out the red carpet."

will be ruled, or you will be speaking this scroll in the spirit in tongues."

I responded, "I deed the territory of this scroll and of the star to the Lord of hosts. Jesus, I commit it to the Lord, and to be the Lord's only."

Stephanie instructed, "Now speak in tongues."

After speaking in tongues for a few moments, Stephanie noted, "Powerful! When you spoke in tongues, the star became long and large with every single word. It became larger and went around as a strip of the tongues went around the entire star. *Do this every day*. I see that it was rolled out, and as you are speaking tongues over it, as if it the next piece of the green carpet roll goes around it, it is just going to keep layering over and over."

Stephanie said, "I call for an angel to bring me my scrolls for my stars. There is a scroll of my personal star, and I deed it completely over to Jehovah. It is Yours.

"I am on my star and as I speak, light is coming out of my mouth. I am seeing myself ahead of time, the next time I do it. Light is coming out of my mouth everywhere like a beam, and it is creating things on my star.

"I ask for the scroll to the second star that I have.

"Moses is with me as if he is showing me something to do. He is just standing there with me. I am to read the scroll and walk on this star. It is like an earthquake under my feet when I walk. It causes the star to grow.

Stephanie said, "Well, I deed this fully to the Lord. I give this star—this territory, and the earthquake under my feet to the Lord Jehovah."

Moses asked, "Wasn't that simple?"

Stephanie replied, "Thank you, Moses for this understanding and revelation."

Speaking to Moses, I asked, "Moses, I have a question for you on that please. What Scripture would we talk about for these stars?"

Moses replied, "It's in 1 John and it's in Revelation."

The 1 John Scripture was given to dispel doubts she had as that moment concerning her ability to hear clearly.

She read:

> *My darling children, you have nothing to fear; do not doubt for a moment the legitimacy of your sonship! You originate in God and have already conquered the worldly religious system because of the unveiling of Christ in you! His living presence in you is far superior to the futile anti-Christ mindsets present in the world! Their conversation mirrors their source and appeals to a common audience. The pseudo claim of a pseudo system has blindfolded multitudes to believe a lie about themselves. (1 John 4:4) (THE MIRROR)*

With that confirmation that she could trust her hearing, she said, "Thank you for that, knowing who I am in Jesus. What Scriptures?"

Moses said, "Call if forward like a scroll."

Stephanie responded, "I call this information forward, like a scroll. Let me see the scroll.

"We are in Revelation 12."

I started at Revelation 12:1,

Suddenly a spectacular symbolic image appears in the sky! A woman clothed in sunlight with a shining moon under her feet and a crown of twelve stars on her head! (THE MIRROR)

I remarked, "Moses, there is a Scripture in Revelation about 'I will give Him the morning star.'[79] Is this what we are learning today?"

Moses replied, "A star is a star, is a star, is a star."

Stephanie said, "Is that a yes?"

Moses said, "You can take that as a yes."

We understood from Moses that this was something we were to do every morning to help command our day. We had been learning about governing our realms and territories and cultivating our landscape, so this was simply an expansion on what we had been learning. I

---

[79] Revelation 2:28

had a question for Moses, "Moses, can I ask about the 1 Corinthians 15 Scriptures?"

> [40] There are also celestial bodies and terrestrial bodies; but the glory of the celestial is one, and the glory of the terrestrial is another. [41] There is one glory of the sun, another glory of the moon, and another glory of the stars; for one star differs from another star in glory.

Moses replied, "The revelation of stars is all through the word. You know what to do with the word study. 1 Corinthians is a path to the knowledge of stars."

Stephanie remarked, "That's why we were on a path this morning! It always comes together."

"Ron, look at that while we are talking about 1 Corinthians 15: 40-41 from the Mirror Translation:

> [40] There are celestial bodies as well as terrestrial bodies. The glory of the one differs from the other. There are skin-bodies and spirit-bodies. [41] The glory of the sun differs from the glory of the moon; [while the one radiates light, the other reflects light.] Also, the stars differ from one another. Each one occupies its own unique place in space. (THE MIRROR)

I remarked, "As we read our scroll, the daily scroll, the path is laid out before us?"

Moses replied, "It enlarges the Kingdom. That is the entire first purpose of it."

I asked, "And if you are having trouble reading it in your language, will praying in tongues take care of that?"

Moses said,

---

*"Praying in the spirit
always brings light.
With every word,
it will be developed."*

I remarked, "This is part of building your territory or governing your territory, and you are landscaping."

Moses replied, "It is part of the Trust of Inheritance."

Stephanie added, "So Moses, that's why this teaching started off about how we had to lay down of our flesh, because our minds can't even grasp this work."

Moses responded, "Now you can see why the co-laboring is of great value. It is not in and of yourselves, but of the Lord. It is *HIS* Kingdom coming. We are each a piece of *HIS* territory."

Stephanie remarked, "When Moses said that, I could see (as people get this revelation knowledge and understanding and do this with more and more people), it was a jigsaw puzzle of a landscape, and pieces were being put in their place, building out and enlarging the Kingdom. This exactly what this is.

> *As we take our place as sons,*
> *utilizing this co-laboring with Heaven,*
> *the vastness of everyone being*
> *able to do that on this planet*
> *would bring about*
> *the Kingdom quickly.*

Especially if we all did it at the same time—simultaneously. That is why we pray in the mornings.

Stephanie continued, "Moses just showed me that on planet earth, my morning is in the evening of someone else's day. That way everything is covered, and all times of day are covered—all mornings. I never thought of that before in that respect.

"I feel like it is the end of our session, but what is interesting is, I must go back through where I came in, as he is having me—just as a point of seeing, go back through from the ocean to the forest, allowing me to see the stone wall and the waterfall where he governs—the place that he stands, that is this very large, vast territory.

"Now I am standing where I was, and behind me is the cavern. I can smell the moisture in the cave, and the portal is still open. Ezekiel has his sword in his hand which is still very large. Now, I am standing in the water, which I am quite enjoying, and he has closed the curtain of water behind us."

Coupling this information with the narrative in the chapter on *The Kingdom Dynamics of Governing Our*

Territory, I could now see the governing attributes of stars that Genesis 1 spoke of. Throughout the Bible are references to stars. We will unpack this more in the next chapter.

Again, it is a subject that you probably won't see unless your eyes have been opened to the concept of it, but once your eyes are opened, they can easily see its repetition is Scripture. More information was to come to help us grasp this revelation and learn to walk in it.

———·———

Chapter 21
The Kingdom Dynamics of Obtaining Our Daily Scroll

We had never seen in the Court of Times and Seasons what we were seeing in this engagement with Heaven. We accessed the Court of Time and Seasons and could see what was essentially, a monthly calendar on the wall and each day had a cubicle in the wall with it. In each cubicle was a scroll. We were instructed that we could access the Court of Times and Seasons, where we could ask the angel for ones' scroll for their star(s) for that day.

In what we were seeing, the attendant in the Court of Times and Seasons had a sheet of paper in his hand containing a list of things. On the list we read, "Night Patrollers, Lasso (but this lasso was big enough to lasso one of the stars we saw), and pipes."

As we continued reading the list, we saw "Verbal Ammunition." This Verbal Ammunition looked like living letters. It is used against a natural verbal onslaught. As we requested these things from the Father, the attendant marked them off the list by placing a check mark by each one.

> *Father, we also request angel food, and elixir. We request Night Patrollers, Lassos, Pipes, and Verbal Ammunition for Ezekiel, his commanders, and ranks.*

Speaking to the angels, we said,

> *Now, in the name of Jesus, we commission you to the full use of the Night Patrollers, the Lassos, the Pipes, and the Verbal Ammunition for the expansion of the Kingdom of God, in Jesus' name.*

Stephanie commented, "Ron, as the attendant was leaving, he showed me quickly that your own personal star and territories are to be governed. You govern because your territories include children and grandchildren, and from your star you can govern their lives."

Ezekiel remarked, "Consider it calling things as if they were."[80]

Stephanie added, "Even though they are not. Where they lay their heads, consider the co-laboring of your territory there. I see it as if you are speaking from your star, and calling things out, calling things in, as if they never were. They are your territories laid on top of theirs

---

[80] Romans 4:17

as a protective covering. I see it as *ordering the day* on their behalf until they get to that place where they can do it on their own, where they walk co-laboring with the angels, but you are going to know this by the reading of the scroll."

Stephanie said, "My question was, can I do that as well, for my own children? But I see this as, we are learning governing of these stars via the scrolls, as Wisdom is present and Holy Spirit, to allow us to know how we can do that without encroaching beyond what we are supposed to. But clearly, we have been given this territory, this help for a reason. It makes sense that our offspring would be on our territories."

I immediately put into practice what I had learned and began governing the territory of my children and grandchildren.

Governing from ones' star is a celestial matter, and although we miss it when reading the Word, Philippians 2 opens the avenue of the celestial. Remember in Philippians 2:10, it says, *Every knee would bow of things above the earth, on the earth, and under the earth.* We are just looking on this plane and what we see with our natural eyes.

Stephanie remarked, "Remember, too, Joseph and his coat of many colors. He had the dream about the stars, with the stars representing each of his brothers."[81]

---

[81] Genesis 37:9

The concept of stars *is* throughout the Bible.

Meeting with George

Our engagement with Moses ended and we asked to check in with George, our financial advisor.

Stephanie described our engagement with him, "We were taken immediately to the Business Complex, given a badge (a lanyard of some sort) and there a woman in white escorted us. We are going to the last hallway on the left, going down this hallway and she is turning us to the right. We came to a vault, and I took the badge and slid it in the slot to access the vault. The person in white began turning a giant wheel on the front of the vault door (like you might see on a bank vault). I just heard it click. It is taking a bit of effort for this woman in white to push the door open. It is that heavy. We entered the vault, and we are standing on gold floors. Every part of the entire floor is gold. I can hear my feet as if I had shoes clicking on this. It is very big. It is more than a room. It is a place of great treasure. Even the walls had various types of treasure hanging on them."

Asking George what we needed to do here, he said, "This is a territory assigned. That is why you saw and felt the vastness of it. Consider this place. Consider the vastness of this place."

Stephanie responded, "Can you tell us, what we need to do? Is there something specific while we are considering this place? I know you are trying to help us understand that these riches are for LifeSpring and that it is very deep and vast. Is there something that needs to be done to bring this vastness into the reality of LifeSpring? Wisdom is sitting near against the wall with George."

Speaking to me, Stephanie said, "I do not know what this place is other than it belongs to LifeSpring.

Wisdom and George were sitting very casually like they were having tea with one another over a casual conversation. There was nothing that seemed urgent."

Again, she asked George, "Is there something we need to do?"

Wisdom replied, "Ron, you have been given three stars to govern from."

Stephanie described her perception, "Now, I am seeing all three stars. I am seeing how the first governs everything—all things that are not as if they were. You are doing this from your territory and from your governing and your rule on your first star (your personal star) as if it is hovering over these other three stars. Call it in Ron. Call in what is needed for the ministry."

I immediately called in a specific amount of money to come into the bank accounts of the ministry without delay, in the name of Jesus.

Stephanie remarked, "George just got up and walked away to do what he needed to do."

Wisdom said, "That that is how you do it, Ron, from your place of governance. Now you are to speak in tongues."

Stephanie attempted to describe what she was seeing as I spoke in tongues over my territory, "I see Heaven has opened portals and treasures are dropping into the portals. Use your lightning bolt! Things are falling from the sky. When Wisdom said, 'Call it in,' she stood up from her chair and although she did not remove herself, it was as if the floor became transparent. Then things on the sides of the walls just began to fall through the portals.

"As you began to speak in tongues, treasures and things that represent treasures such as gold, jewels, stoles came from the vault through the portal to the earth." Stephanie added, "We request this in time, out of time, and ahead of time, in Jesus' name."

Governing realms, territories, and dimensions is the lot of the sons of God. Isaiah 9:6 foretold this with a passage we typically attribute to only be speaking of Jesus.

> [1] *Nevertheless, the gloom will not be upon her who is distressed, as when at first, He lightly esteemed the land of Zebulun and the land of Naphtali, and afterward more heavily oppressed her, by the way of the sea, beyond the Jordan, in Galilee of the Gentiles.* [2] *The people who walked in darkness have seen a great light (the sons of God arising); those who dwelt in the land of the shadow of death, upon them a light has shined.* [3] *You have*

multiplied the nation and increased its joy; they rejoice before you according to the joy of harvest, as men rejoice when they divide the spoil.

⁴ For You have broken the yoke of his burden and the staff of his shoulder, the rod of his oppressor, as in the day of Midian. ⁵ For every warrior's sandal from the noisy battle, and garments rolled in blood, will be used for burning and fuel of fire.

⁶ For unto us a child (Jesus) is born, unto us a son (the bene *sons of God) is given; and the government will be upon His shoulder. And His name will be called Wonderful, Counselor, Mighty God, Everlasting Father, Prince (Steward/Keeper) of Peace. ⁷ Of the increase of His government and peace there will be no end, upon the throne of David and over His kingdom, to order it and establish it with judgment and justice from that time forward, even forever. The zeal of the Lord of hosts will perform this." (Isaiah 9:1-7) (Emphasis added)*

What we have attributed as only being the work of Jesus in the earth may also be that of including the governing of the sons in the earth. Government is upon our shoulders, not just the shoulders of Jesus. We are the stewards of peace in the earth.

I had heard a vague reference to our personal star from Malcolm (the man in white, our frequent tutor) who had mentioned it on one occasion with no explanation.

In Matthew 2:1-2, we read that Jesus had a star—His personal star.

> *"Now after Jesus was born in Bethlehem of Judea in the days of Herod the king, behold, wise men from the East came to Jerusalem, ² saying, "Where is He who has been born King of the Jews? For we have seen **His** star in the east and have come to worship Him." (Emphasis added)*

This was mentioned several times in the story of His birth.

Paul speaks of the glory (illumination) of one star will differ from the illumination (glory) of another star.[82] Each star reflects the Glory its owner carries. Much glory brings much illumination. The glory can be increased by praying out the scroll of that star—both in the spirit and in the natural.

In Revelation 1, He appears with seven stars of the seven churches. Jesus himself had the morning star (Revelation 2:28). When it speaks of the stars falling to the earth in Revelation 6:13, it speaks of the authority of that star being no more. It became as dust. The falling to earth of the stars is not a literally falling to earth as a meteor would do. Stars represent authority and the authority had been forfeited by the seven churches.

---

[82] 1 Corinthians 15:40

The woman in Revelation 12:1 appeared with 12 stars which represented governmental dominion that had been given to her—essentially by the church by default.

Finally, Jesus is announced as the bright and morning star in Revelations 22:6.

Amos 5:6 refers to a star of a false god. This is repeated several times in the Old Testament. Could this be a concept that is so obvious that we overlook it in our reading of Scripture? It would appear so. The verse quoted earlier from Matthew 2:2 tells us plainly that Jesus had a personal star. If he had more than one star, I do not know. It was significant that Magi from east came to worship where they were led by that star.

Abraham was told his descendants would be a numerous as the sand on the seashore and the stars in the skies. Each of us has a personal star, and stars always had a governmental aspect to them in Scripture.

Malcolm and others have been teaching us about governing realms, territories and even dimensions. This teaching from Moses brought it even closer to home. He explained that we have a personal star where we are to govern from. For us, LifeSpring has several stars relating to different aspects of our ministry. Not only do each of *us* have a star, we have territories also which we are to govern over. We will be learning more about this in the next few chapters.

Chapter 22
The Kingdom Dynamics of Piercing the Veil of Orphanhood

Stephanie and I had engaged Heaven and were in the upstairs conference room where one wall is clear and we can see stars and galaxies. Malcolm was with us and he took what we would think of as a laser pointer pen and he pointed to a star, far off in the galaxy, and then he drew a line to another star. When he did, it created a permanent red line from one star to the next. Then he did it again to other stars. At first, I thought he was going to try to recreate one of the constellations, but that's not what was happening. We wondered why he was pinpointing this one star in relation to all the others. Some understanding came.

In governance, all stars are relatable. Stars are relevant to governance in that it doesn't matter the distance between them. Our stars are in different places quantumly. In the vision, the second star, that I would have considered the one in a different quantum realm, is a place of *governing in the future*. It looked like our future governance of things **relationally** to how we saw the first elder and John the Baptist.[83]

The first star was Stephanie's personal star, containing her personal landscape and her personal territories, that she can govern. To Stephanie, it felt as if she was governing from the second star even though it was in the spiritual realm. The first star had more of a personal feel.

The second star was a governance outside of her personal star, on behalf of the Kingdom. But her personal star will be in a relational place when she steps dimensionally and quantumly to govern with the other star.

That is why he showed that it didn't matter how far they were apart dimensionally or quantumly. There is a relational aspect to each one of them.

The Bright and Morning Star

Jesus is the Bright and Morning Star. That is where He rules from. That is His governance. *It is a sonship matter*. Jesus knows He is God's son and as the Bright and Morning Star, rules from that place. He governs from that place.

---

[83] We had engaged with one of the elders in a prior engagement with Heaven and on another occasion with John the Baptist.

*Do you believe you are
just as much a son as Jesus,
with capabilities of governance?*

These are positional matters to the Father.

*Take your position as sons
that you may govern,
co-laboring with His Word,
His will, His nature—
yes, His very nature.*

Many reflect on their lack of authority in the natural realm, but it is because they are deflecting it or reflecting it from that realm. Authority is a governance.

*The sons must know
they are sons in order to son.*

It is more than the time and place where we will learn about how we govern; it is the time and place to learn to be sons.

Piercing the Veil of Orphanhood[84]

This revelation will pierce the veil that is the darkness of orphanhood.

Did you know that the word orphan is from the vocabulary of hell? No one—not one, is an orphan. They are sons.

The word "orphan," or the phrase "orphan mentality" that people have when they lose their natural parents, was a word that ends up being an entity that people take on. They are blinded by the *orphanhood,* bringing the feeling of being abandoned by their Heavenly Father or having that feeling because they have lost their natural parents. But Heaven is saying no one—not even one, is an orphan.

The Father is calling His sons to stand and to take their places as sons.

It is how the Kingdom of Heaven works—His Kingdom come; His will be done. This is His will. This is His Kingdom.

---

[84] See the prayer template for *Overturning the Curse of the Bastard, Curse of the Eunuch, and Curse of Alienation* at the end of this chapter.

Walking with Wisdom

Then Malcolm sat down, and Wisdom came in and reminded us to invoke her at every turn. In every revelation, invoke her. Wisdom will show the way. She will help illuminate the path.

When we, "invoke wisdom," we are not *just* invoking Wisdom, but all the Seven Spirits of God. It may feel like they are separate, but they are also one.

As an act of faith, we invoked Wisdom and the Seven Spirits, and we took our stand and position as a son, with our stars that were activated and where our scrolls were read. We thought of it relationally with the other star in quantum.

We thank You, Father, that being a son is so much bigger than our minds could ever think or imagine. We thank You. We had no idea of what has been stolen from us. We have been lied to and told we are orphans and that you have abandoned us. Thank you for truth.

Wisdom, we ask that you illuminate the path, in Jesus' name.

As soon as we asked that, it was as if from the upper conference room, the path was illuminated from this room straight out to the star that we could see in the distance. As Stephanie stepped onto the path and took a step off what seemed like a platform, she was immediately in front of her star.

Our first step off the platform was to meet the star even though we, in a manner of speaking, met them in the prior engagement. This day our scrolls were read.

We said, "Wisdom, I invoke you at every turn and your revelation. I invoke you and ask that you show me the way. I ask you to illuminate my path and teach me how to govern from my stars."

Meeting Our Star

As we both had been introduced to our stars, Stephanie saw me take a step and suddenly, I was at one of my stars.

We each greeted our star (remember, it is an entity, it has sentience. When Stephanie spoke to her star it spoke back saying, "Hello Stephanie."

I pointed out to her that her star also has a name. She said she was going to need to sit on that for a minute.

Her star pointed out that not all stars had been named by humans. Her star also pointed out that he would also be teaching her how to govern from her star. Stars want to be governed in the morning hours before one's day begins in earnest.

Each government is specific to each spirit. Her star pointed out, "There are many stars that will come into alignment because of you."

Stephanie added, "When he said, 'you,' it's in this position that I'm in with LifeSpring. So, it has everything to do with LifeSpring Ministries. I would imagine your star is going to say something similar. When you said alignment, it is like a correction in time or something. I see my star and then I see another star here and another star here and another star here (pointing to different places), and when he said alignment, they all came into the same position together in alignment."

For this revelation to be unpacked and received, we were going to need the work of Awakening Angels.

> *I call Awakening Angels to come.*
>
> *I commission Awakening Angels from this place that I govern and where I am learning to govern from this place, I commission you, Awakening Angels to go and awaken those that are my family members, my lineage, and those that I will touch in this ministry and through this ministry.*
>
> *I commission you to awaken the saints to the existence of their stars and to the part that they play in the governing of realms and governing of dimensions, in the name of Jesus.*

We were learning intuitively that one of the purposes of praying in the spirit is when you cannot perceive what is on your scroll, your spirit already knows, and it helps unlock it to us.

Praying in the spirit unveils things for us.

Although our mind may not always perceive it, our spirit will.

It is why the enemy stole speaking in tongues from the church, polluted the knowledge of it, and scared people with it. What a force to be reckoned with if we all prayed in the spirit.

Remember when Abraham was given the promise about descendants—as many as the sands of the seashore and the *stars* in the sky.

In my book, *Engaging Angels from the Realms of Heaven*, I discuss engaging with our angels to patrol our realms. We then learned about commissioning our angels to certain tasks. Now, we are learning to do more than engage or commission our angels, we are learning to govern the realms we have jurisdiction over as well as governing territories and stars. These revelations have been progressively unveiled over the last few years. As we engage and co-labor with our angels, Wisdom, and the other Seven Spirits of God, as well as with men and women in white, we will see the Kingdom expanded in our life in new measures. Treasures of revelation and provision will open over our life and direction and authority will become clearer and more powerful as we walk out being a son living from the Kingdom Dynamics of Heaven.

Prayer Template For Overturning The Curse Of The Bastard, Curse Of The Eunuch, And Curse Of Alienation From The Lord

Father, in the name of Jesus, I request access to Your Courts. I enter in with praise and thanksgiving because You have given me access to these heavenly realms through Jesus. I request access to the Court of Appeals to request the overturning of false verdicts (those established by Satan and Courts of Hell) and the establishment of righteous ones.

I enter today on behalf of _____ (myself, or the name of the person you are praying for) and my (their) bloodline ancestry, all the way back to the hand of the Father.

I confess as sin the activities of my ancestors who engaged in sexual perversion. I confess as sin where these activities became the iniquity of sexual perversion in my bloodline. I repent for those in my bloodline generations who willingly and knowingly, or unwillingly and unknowingly, engaged in adultery, of any form and with any gender in any timeline, in time or out of time, in any age, realm, or dimension, all the way back to the hand of the Father and as far forward as it needs to go.

I confess as sin and repent for the sin of selfishness, rebellion, and self-idolatry connected to this sexual sin.

I confess as sin and repent for the sin of physical or emotional abandonment of covenant spouses.

I confess as sin and repent for all illegitimate births within the bloodline that gave rise to children and seed falling into the curse of the bastard.

I confess as sin and repent for the sin of those who engaged in all fornication, incest, and rape in homosexual or lesbian behaviors.

I confess as sin and repent for the sin of those engaged in sexual self-mutilation, or the mutilation of others, and all transgender behavior.

I confess as sin and repent for the sin of any who operated in pedophilia and other aberrant sexual conduct of every flavor.

I confess as sin and repent for those in my generations, both in my paternal and maternal bloodlines, who operated in those behaviors and encouraged others to do the same things.

I repent for the originating sin within these bloodlines.

I confess and repent of my own sin in these matters as well.

I agree with You and Your Word about these activities and deeds and confess the sins of my ancestors when they engaged in them. I repent of them on their behalf.

With the intent of my will, I choose to forgive the humans who were and are responsible for introducing this into the family line. I forgive them, bless them, and release them from guilt, in the name of Jesus. I ask You to forgive them, too. I ask You to put these sins under the Blood of Jesus in all my family's ancestral bloodlines. I ask for the blood of Jesus to cleanse me and my bloodlines of this sin and these iniquities.

With regard to this sin and iniquity in my bloodline, I request that every false verdict resulting from these sins and iniquities be overturned by this Court. I request the release of every human captive, with their soul and spirit parts, to be released from these false verdicts and be released from any resulting evil trading floors and evil trade routes, to be granted a righteous verdict based upon my plea for the Blood of Jesus to cover me and my bloodline's ancestors and generations. I ask for the collapse of all evil trading floors and trade routes that were opened by these ancestral sins.

As an amendment to this case, and in the Court of Cancellations, I am requesting the full cancellation of the curse of the bastard and the curse of the eunuch for me and my bloodlines and generations. I am requesting the cancellation of the curse of not being allowed into the assembly of the Lord. I enter into this Court my confession and repentance completed just now and on record in the Court of Appeals.

I ask You, Just Judge, to cleanse this curse from me, from my spirit, soul, and body by the washing of the water of the Word, the Living Water, and the Blood of Jesus. I ask You to cleanse this curse and its effects from me and my family line and in me, my generations, and my future generations as well as from all our DNA. I ask You to release me and all those related to me by blood, marriage, adoption or civil and religious covenant from these curses and from the consequences, impacts, and ramifications of these curses.

I also request restitution to me and anyone else affect by the negative consequences of this curse. I request the complete restoration of my spiritual nearness to You, to Jesus, and to Holy Spirit. I ask that I may worship You in Spirit and in Truth from now going forth. I ask for a verdict of the complete annulment of these curses.

As an amendment to this court case, I request entry into the Presence of the Lord and into the times of His refreshing for myself, my generations, and my future generations.

———— · ————

Chapter 23

The Kingdom Dynamics of Spiritual Authority & Governing

As we engaged Heaven, a woman in white wearing an extremely elegant gown greeted us. We asked her name, she answered, "Diane." She was going to assist us in our engagement with Heaven. As we followed her, Stephanie noticed her earrings which were pearls.

Stephanie remarked, "Oh, you're wearing pearls of wisdom." We could sense she was Wisdom's friend.

We came to a large open space. It seemed like a ballroom, but Diane clarified and said it was a banquet hall. Noticing the grand staircase to the right, she saw images of lampstands that are like those described in the Holy of Holies. There were two of them flanking either side of two massive double doors. We were about to walk in, and as we opened the door, Stephanie heard it click as it unlocked.

Stephanie said, "Diane, I feel like I'm stuck right here. Is there something I should say or do to be able to step into this place?"

Diane replied, "Smell the aroma."

Stephanie remarked, "It smells to me like fresh baked bread."

Diane said, "Sense."

Stephanie explained, "She's meaning using the senses. It felt like a spray, like mist of mostly air with tiny flecks of water."

Diane then said, "Now see."

As Stephanie looked up, she described what she was seeing, "There's a very large table and there are a lot of people around it and they are feasting—and when I say large, there might be 50 people at this table or more."

She suddenly realized where we were and said, "We are at John's place in Heaven where he governs from." She was referring to the Apostle John who wrote the book of John.

She saw John from across the room and he came up to her and greeted her. He had a full beard that was very dark and black. She noted how jolly he was.

Stephanie greeted him. He had a gold cup in his left hand, and grapes in his right hand. As Stephanie was going to extend her hand to shake his hand, he instead grabbed her and hugged her.

She said, "John, it is very nice to meet you."

Spiritual Authority & Governing

He replied, "Spiritual Authority. It's something, isn't it?"

Stephanie remarked, "It is."

John commented, "It's *not* so serious."

Stephanie explained, "I realize what he means. He's talking about that religious spirit that can make things so very serious. What I'm seeing is a feast, and I'm seeing the enjoyment of people—not seriousness. I'm seeing celebration (while they are governing)."

John said, "I am doing it from my place of governance and spiritual authority."

Stephanie remarked, "John, I think what you're trying to tell me is, yes, there is a place and a time to be in that seriousness of the work, but ruling in governance and spiritual authority also means celebration and joy."

Stephanie continued, "All of a sudden, the room stayed the same, but all the people were gone except for one. The one person he was showing me was in the banquet hall, even though *they were ALSO in* their own spiritual dimension, governing and ruling *from* that place, and they were able to be celebrating with him *at the same time—quantumly*. Then John showed me, as more and more people began to be added to the table, that *that's* what they were doing, too. They are in AND *on* their own territory, in their own realm and dimension doing what they're supposed to be doing, in governance, but at the same time, they were in the banquet hall celebrating with John."

John said, "We're celebrating the resurrected King, but we are doing it from *our* seat of authority—governing."

Speaking to John, Stephanie said, "This goes back to what we were taught about 'projection' isn't it? Initially, when we were taught about governing, Heaven said, 'Consider a projection,' meaning, we could project our thought and then be there. Am I correct?"

John replied, "What are you doing right now? Not only are you quantumly at work, but you're also protectively at work. You're in a seat in your home, and yet you are here in front of me!"

John explained, "You have made a choice to interact. You have made a choice to step in, and you have made a choice to trade. You have made a choice to be open, and you have made a choice to celebrate. *Stephanie, you are already governing.*"

***You** are already governing!*

Stephanie continued, "And just like that, we are being pulled away from the scene. She called out, "Bye John!"

Stephanie described, "As I am being pulled away from the scene, I'm watching all of them celebrate and the doors are closing in front of me. Ron, they are letting us know that *we are already governing*. It's not a future thing. We are already doing it."

Stephanie remarked, "Everyone is going to be so excited. What they're showing us is the simplicity, right? It not far reaching, *we're already doing it*."

Stephanie exclaimed, "That was our appointment. It just dawned on me. We had an appointment with John!" That morning when we checked in with Heaven, we had a limited amount of time to engage, but Heaven mentioned an appointment was on our calendar for that day which is why we did this engagement with Heaven although we did not know if this was the appointment Heaven was referring to earlier in the day.

Stephanie continued, "I feel like I should describe the room. The table was long. It was made of wood, and it reminded me that our Jesus was a carpenter and He loved to create things. I can imagine that He had created this table especially for John. It had bench seating and no chairs. John was not at the table, because his table was full, but he was in a chair in what we would think of as a corner. Everything behind it was open air and grass and trees. He had gotten up out of that chair and he had a fist full of grapes and a cup in the other hand when he came over to greet me. There was such celebration."

---

*We often forget
that our spirit never sleeps.*

While our body is sleeping and our soul is resting, our spirit is on excursions throughout the universe and beyond. We can't yet fathom just how much exists around us.

As a matter of stewardship, Heaven would have us learn about governing realms from our earliest times in walking with Him.

We learn to discipline ourselves by waking in the morning and going about our day. We learn to discipline our body in dietary matters which is practicing governing. How we do will vary from day to day or year to year, but as we learn to operate the Law of Exchange, which is to exchange on thing for another of value to you, that too, is practicing governing. Heaven has been training us in governing throughout our lives. However, to govern in the natural does not mean we understand governing via the spirit. Some of the principles are the same, but the applications are very different. The engagements with Heaven are expanding our understanding of just how much we will be learning in our lessons on governing our realms, territories, domains, and dimensions. The excitement never ends!

Chapter 24
The Kingdom Dynamics of Expectancy

In this engagement, we were met by Ezekiel. We have discovered that Ezekiel can be very serious and at other times, rather jovial. Stephanie described this day in this manner, "Ezekiel is here, and he has a paper airplane in his right hand. He is just flying it around while holding it with his fingers like you would see a small child do." She said, "I'm not sure what that's about." She decided to ask Ezekiel, "Why is that in your hand, Ezekiel? What is it for?"

Ezekiel replied, "Buckle your seat belts."

Stephanie commented, "He just handed me a seatbelt." She took it from him and buckled up. He also had one for me to buckle as well.

Ezekiel remarked, "It's going to be a bumpy ride." Then he leaned in and said, "Not really."

Stephanie remarked, "We get it. It's going to be something! We are walking and are now in what would have been the upper-level conference room where the large window that we usually could see the galaxies from was open. I just stepped off the ledge, and it's as if I'm walking on air, but I feel something solid underneath my feet. As we're walking, we're being flanked by a lot of angels. A lot of angels are walking with us. I can hear their feet. It reminds me of movies where you've heard the Roman soldiers marching in cadence. We stopped, and it was as if what we were walking on would be considered glass but there is nothing on either side of this walkway on the left or the right except angels. The angels just stopped, and they jumped off the sides and are flying with their wings." Stephanie asked, "Ezekiel, can you tell me what they're doing?"

Harvest Time

Ezekiel replied, "This is about the harvest. This is harvest time. I know you think of harvest as those the Lord is going to save, but harvest means many more things.

There is a completion in a matter and the harvest has come.

"For those that have been prayed in excellence, the harvest has come. For those that have faithfully sought, asked, and knocked, the harvest has come. These angels you see are the Delivering Angels, delivering the harvest of what the Lord has for His people—songs, knowledge, words, expectations:

Expect the unexpected.

"Truths are being delivered, and so are faith, hope, love, as well as miracle signs and wonders. The pathway forward is cleared. There are no obstructions.

The calling of 'open wide the gates'—
that is this day.

He asked, "Have you had an earnest expectation, Stephanie?"

Stephanie replied, "I have."

Ezekiel responded, "Then expect His Kingdom to come, His will be done. You think that quantum matters shook your mind. These honest expectations far exceed those, for this is directly from the hand of the Father to His people. Expect the unexpected."

Stephanie said, "Ezekiel, Ron and I—we expect the unexpected.

Father, we thank You. We thank You for this day. Thank You that You have made the path cleared for this day. For the people. For Your sons.

Receiving Your Inheritance

Stephanie remarked, "Now my vision has been increased about what the angels are doing. I see so many of them, but they are going to different places. I'm assuming this is Heaven or in different quantum places, and they are picking things that are treasures—that are gifts. This is the inheritance. There are pieces of the inheritance. They are picking up, and they are bringing it. I see portals open everywhere below me, everywhere! And they are dipping in and delivering these things.

"I have an angel that just came in front of me with two keys on a ring. I'm going to take them."

"Thank you, angel," she remarked. She asked the angel, "What do I do with these?"

She gained the impression to slip them on her wrist.

She continued, "I have another angel that showed up that has two scrolls. I will take those. 'Thank you.' I have put them in my heart.

"I also have an angel that came in and a door was in front of him. He just kicked the door open. 'Thank you, angels.'

"I have another angel that just came in that laid down a lot of tan bags in front of me. 'Thank you, angel.'"

Ezekiel said, "Now see, Ron. See what you have been brought."

Stephanie said, "It's an angel with a sword. Ron, it's your sword. It's very large. There is also an angel with an illuminated pathway that he just put in front of you. Another angel came and planted two trees, one on each side of the pathway. As you enter to walk on that illuminated pathway, you'll see two trees on either side. There's an angel that has brought different body parts for healing purposes. I see organs and I see a leg."

The angel spoke saying, "A decree from the Father—with long life shall I satisfy you."

Stephanie continued, "I see keys being brought to Adina. They are bringing a scroll. An instruction is being brought to David along with vats of oil—anointing oil or some substance is being given to David, and it is permeating his home.

"A general's badge or pin is being given to Jeremy.[85] A microphone and a platform are being given to Joyce. Very broad wings are being fashioned onto Kevin's back—just these feathers and wings. There are these beautiful, little girl dresses being given to Karee so that she can step in as a little girl and sit on Papa's lap.[86] Very clearly, I see it.

"There are so many more things being given to people that are part of our ministry—to those that draw close to the ministry. I just see all these portals open, and they are bringing things so quickly that it is amazing. It's like

---

[85] Jeremy is one of our team members.
[86] Joyce, Kevin, and Karee are some of our Senior Advocates.

when they gather up and they bring it, they go and gather more and bring it, and gather more and bring it. Each portal feels like they are representative of those who belong to this ministry and their family members."

Finally, Stephanie asked, "What am I looking at?"

Ezekiel replied, "On behalf of the King, His will is being done for His sons, they are receiving their inheritance."

Stephanie responded, "It's because of trades, isn't it?"

Ezekiel said, "It's because you are sons."

Stephanie replied, "Amen! Now my focus is back staying in front of Ezekiel. I know that the angels are still working below us.

She said, "Father, we commend Ezekiel with his commanders and ranks and patrols. For the work that they are doing for the sons, we request an honoring of them. We honor them and the work that they do on Your behalf. We request angel food, bread, and elixir."

Ezekiel continued, "It's more than just what I mentioned. There are things like beauty for ashes being delivered."

Stephanie replied, "It's a beautiful picture, Ezekiel. Thank you. Ezekiel, I ask that you, your commanders, and ranks would co-labor, on behalf of all of those having these things being brought to them, with their angels, to bring these things to their realms that they might know the favor of the Lord."

Ezekiel commented, "Testimonies are coming."

Stephanie said, "We give all the glory to God."

With that, Ezekiel left to be a part of what was going on.

———·———

Chapter 25
The Kingdom Dynamics of Governing from Our Star

Stephanie noted, "Wisdom is here, and she is addressing you, Ron."

Wisdom asked, "Would you like me to illuminate the path to your stars to govern what was just released to the people that are upon the territory of LifeSpring Ministries?"

Stephanie explained, "There's an illuminated path in front of you. In the spirit, step off, and Wisdom is going to take you."

I followed the instruction, and Stephanie described what she observed, "You are on your personal star and there is a path for the other three. Then there is a connection between the three as you stand on your star. This one is connected to the three. It's relational. Wisdom is reminding you about that."

Wisdom said, "From this place, you will govern what are the stars of LifeSpring that touch the territories of those that draw near to the ministry."

Stephanie asked, "Wisdom, can you show us how he needs to do that?"

Wisdom responded, "Pause for just a moment, Ron, and experience the relationship with all of those that draw near. This is relational. You are the apostle over them."

Stephanie continued, "There are scrolls now in front of you, Ron. You are suspended in space and all these scrolls are in front of you. They are the scrolls that belong to each person because you have authority over a piece of their territory, as their apostle. As the one over LifeSpring you can commission the angels from this place as a governing, to bring those scrolls to each one."

I began,

In the name of Jesus, I commission the angels of each of these individuals to deliver their scrolls to them to the enlargement of the Kingdom of Heaven.

Wisdom replied, "Now wasn't that easy?"

Stephanie commented, "It feels like, Wisdom, that from this place there is a different authority than what we've done in the past where we have commissioned the angels to do things."

Wisdom said, "Now commission the people to awaken."

I said,

I commission the people associated with LifeSpring to awaken, in the name of Jesus.

Wisdom replied, "Now that's governance. Now govern and command the enemy to take his hands off the people."

In the name of Jesus, I command Satan and all his forces to take their hands off the people—those that are connected to LifeSpring in any fashion in the name of Jesus.

Stephanie added, "And Wisdom, we invoke you at every turn in this matter."

Wisdom replied, "That's governing from your place of authority. From this place, you can govern."

Stephanie added, "It's as if she's telling me to do this, so, let's do this little test. What is a concern that you have about one of the people that have drawn near to LifeSpring?

Wisdom instructed, "Govern that situation."

I thought of a team member and spoke to their spirit to come alongside LifeSpring and not be opposing us, in the name of Jesus. I then blessed that person to do so.

Stephanie noted, "There is a power from this place doing that. Wisdom, I would like for you to illuminate my path to my star for the scroll."

As she was making her request, the scroll was put around her star.

She said, "Now I have the scroll for the other star. I am to plant it. I am going to dig a hole in the star, and I am going to plant it and ask for living water to water it. From here, I say,

> *No weapon formed against me or my family or those brothers and sisters in Christ that I'm associated with, shall prosper and every tongue that rises against us in judgment, is condemned. From this place that has been deeded to the Lord, I govern my territories that touch the territory of my husband, and my children, and my family. I command the enemy saying, 'You have to leave.' I enforce this, in Jesus' name.*

Stephanie continued, "A whole lot more is coming regarding this. I can see it. It is like a timing thing right now. There will be so much more regarding you, Ron, governing from this place and the understanding of it. What a gift. There are thousands of portals open."

Governing Another's Territory

Concerning another situation we were amid, we were advised, "Ron, govern _____'s territory. It can be sent into the camp of those in the natural coming against her."

I immediately began,

> *In the name of Jesus, I govern _____'s territory and that of _____ and _____. I call confusion into the camp of the enemy. Those that would harass her and try to disturb her peace. I call confusion even into <u>her opponent's</u> life. You'll not mess with her. You will keep your mouth shut. You will not manipulate or control her or the situation in any fashion and neither will you a try to cut off funds from her so that she can't even support _____ and _____that you've taken responsibility for, in the name of Jesus. You will straighten up and fly right, in Jesus' name.*

Stephanie remarked, "I felt that when you were speaking, all I could see was the sound, and I had this revelation. That's exactly how the enemy uses agents, human agents, to speak the sound.

"Because Satan has given them a level of authority that they think that they have, but this is so much greater than that. I saw it as a reverberation on top of the earth. I don't know. It's big, because as it was you spoke to each one of their spirits, Wisdom just showed me a picture of when that atomic bomb goes off, how the reverberation around it destroys everything in its path---that's what you just did. It feels like wielding a sword to me."

As sons, we can govern the territories of those in alignment with us.

Chapter 26
The Kingdom Dynamics of Obedience

As we began our engagement with Heaven, Stephanie remarked, "I immediately hear the song, 'Trust and obey for there's no other way to be happy in Jesus, but to trust and obey.' Heaven had me write it down. 'Trust and obey for there's no other way.' Whoever is singing has a lovely voice. 'Oh hi!' It's Lydia! She's singing it again. What do you want to show us about 'Trust and Obey?'"[87]

Meeting Adam

"We are walking, and we are in a type of garden. It is more than a garden. Someone takes care of this garden. As soon as I said, 'Someone takes care of this garden,'

---

[87] *Trust and Obey* by John Henry Sammis with Music by Daniel Brink Towner.

Adam appeared. He's singing that song, too, and this garden has sculpted plants and beautiful flowers. He's pruning a bush. He is singing, but he has his back to us."

Adam began, "A pleasure to make your acquaintance, Ron and Stephanie."

I said, "Likewise." (Stephanie was speechless.)

Stephanie finally said, "It is our honor, Adam." Then she remarked, "He is strikingly handsome, and he has translucent skin."

Adam remarked, "This is how I looked when I made my steps upon the earth."

Stephanie remarked, "Adam, I'm so glad to be here with you. Our hearts are open to what it is you must share from the Lord and from your own experiences."

Adam asked, "You've learned a lot about trusts, haven't you?"

Stephanie replied, "We have learned about the trusts that the Father has given us, the Trusts of Heaven."

Adam asked, "What about the word 'obey?'"

Stephanie remarked, "Well, I've learned about it my whole life, and I'm very interested to hear what you have to tell us about the word 'obey.'"

He began singing the song again.

Adam said, "'Trust and obey for there is there's no other way.' There is great significance in that song. I wish I had that song in my heart back in the day I walked the earth, but the fact is, the significance of those words, 'Trust and obey for there is no other way'—there *is* no other way."

---

*Obedience is a straight path,
an open way, a marker, an ability
to open a portal—a kingly portal.*

Stephanie commented, "The only way I can describe this, Ron, is he's very lighthearted about his and Eve's role in what happened with humanity."

Adam continued, "You see where disobedience got *us*. I am the first Adam, but Jesus, *the Way, the Truth, and the Life*, has redeemed me—ME, the first Adam.

---

*His obedience
trumps my disobedience
and has provided the access
to all things that are
Kingdom dynamics.*

"Obedience goes beyond the spiritual, religious mindsets of man. This is obedience of the heart—the heart of the matter. This isn't the brow beating of religious tyranny about obedience. This is the wanting to hear of the voice of the Lord and to act upon it. That is obedience. It's an action.

"Look at this garden. I till it today because I want to. I lost that ability. My favorite place, the garden that was created for me to walk upon, that I lived and moved and had my being in, it has been restored to me because of Jesus' obedience."

Stephanie noted, "He just picked up a crown and put it upon his head."

Adam continued, "In spite of the disobedience, because Father restores all things, He gave me a crown of obedience. I made many trades with Heaven, where I traded in righteousness and because of those times, because of those days, the multiplicity has been given back to me *here*. This is my territory. I govern and rule from here. I am a kingly priest because the Father has said that I am. If I can be redeemed—which I have been—the one that all creation can say *caused the fall*, how much more for you in your obedience to the voice of Father? His pulling, His groanings and laboring, and loving on your behalf. Seek these things."

Stephanie replied, "Adam, thank you. Thank you for your story. I saw many things while you were speaking—specifically the reality that, because of the disobedience done that day, all of creation has felt it and yet you stand here, crown upon your head, crowned by the King of Kings, giving the simple example of the Godly trades before the fall that you made count. You showed us that walking in obedience is only way—there is no other way—and when we do this, when we choose an act of obedience, which is a choice, that all these realms, dimensions, and times will be open to us as a portal. Is there anything else you would like to teach us? I appreciate you."

She said, "He's gone back to singing that song and he's working on this beautiful plant—this flower."

Adam added, "I got to name all of these, too!"

Stephanie remarked, "I was thinking I had never seen any of these kinds of flowers before. Thank you, Adam, for your time."

Lydia appeared and took us back to the upper-level conference room.

Obedience—Better than Sacrifice

Stephanie said, "That was pretty amazing, Lydia, thank you for the introduction."

Lydia remarked, "Obedience is better than sacrifice. A better word for obedience is the assurance that your steps walk in accordance with the will of the Father."

Stephanie replied, "Obedience is the assurance of the ordered steps."

Lydia continued,

> *When you trust and obey the Father, your steps are ordered. They are assured.*

Stephanie remarked, "Lydia, I think a lot of people get caught up in the word obedience. We have been brow beaten so hard with that word. It has become such a religious word. I don't like it very much myself, but this new concept, this way of thinking about it, is much easier. Is there anything else you want to share about that in particular?"

Lydia commented, "Why wouldn't Satan distort that word by making it feel hard and un-accomplishable when truly, it's the easiest path? It's so easy. *Anything else* feels hard."

Stephanie replied, "Thank you, Lydia." Lydia left, but we were still sitting in the conference room.

Expect! Expect! Expect!

I suggested, "Let's check with Ezekiel and see if he needs anything."

Ezekiel came in and Stephanie noted, "You have two bags over your shoulder, I see. Is that from yesterday's accomplishments?"

He replied, "Yesterday was accomplished, today is another day."

Stephanie remarked, "Well, thank you for today's accomplished work of capture."

Ezekiel said, "Expect!"

Stephanie asked, "Can you expound upon that word?"

Ezekiel explained saying, "Expect! Expect the unexpected. Expect the growth. Expect the transformation from on high, The seeds have come to fruition. You will see this harvest. Expect the calming of the storm."

Stephanie replied, "We do. Thank you."

Ezekiel continued, "Expect misalignment to be maligned."

Puzzled at what had Ezekiel said, I explained to Stephanie, "When you malign something, you distort its character, so misalignment is being maligned. The misalignment is being corrected."

Stephanie replied, "Thank you, Ezekiel. You may go take those bags and just do with them whatever it is supposed to be done.

I added, "And we do request for you some blue flavored elixir."

Stephanie added, "Blue flavor, yes, and bread—angel bread, and angel food for you, your commanders, and your troops, and your patrollers. Yes, and every armament of Heaven that you need."

———·———

Chapter 27

The Kingdom Dynamics of Engaging from Within Our Star

Just as we have experienced in our many engagements with Heaven, we will start in one place and end up in an entirely different place. Along the way, we are learning concepts that build toward the next one. Today was no different. We were in a room with a lot of people. It wasn't hectic, but the air was filled with excitement. Ezekiel was present and he was showing a mighty beast that had been slain. It was a dragon of some sort, and Ezekiel was showing it to this cloud of witnesses. We knew from a prior engagement that he had been warring with a mighty beast, and now he had finalized the victory over it. Ezekiel said, "The mightier they are, the harder they fall." He was standing just a few feet from the dragon with a lasso in his hand that was roped around the neck of the beast.

We asked for information concerning this and he jokingly said, "Well, I know you've heard about being slain in the spirit."

Malcolm walked up and began to explain by asking a question, "Would you say that, as a Christian, you've been taught many things that just aren't a hundred percent correct?"

We began walking through the crowd and Malcolm continued, "It is true, the mightier the beast, the harder they fall. This is an example. If He who lives inside of you has done this very thing (conquered), why have so many put this outside of their understanding when "greater is He, that is in you, than he that is in the world"? Just simply stating "He is a Conquering King" and not understanding its concept, is futile. Ron has taught you well in that the Lord does what He pleases. Humanity, co-laboring with the Kingdom that is within them, will cause the slaying of *many* mighty beasts. How odd that we walk the face of the earth mindlessly saying, 'The Kingdom of Heaven is within me.' *He **is** a mighty Conquering King* and yet, there is no belief in that, no real belief that happens in an individual's life. This is part of *laying down oneself*. This is part of understanding that you truly are not doing anything in and of yourselves. You *can* believe that the Lord is slaying your enemies. He *is* preparing a table in the presence of your enemies. This Kingdom Principle is imperative for the sons to walk in new levels of understanding. How can you walk in quantum if you can't even walk as sons? He *is* the Conquering King. Love conquers all. That mighty beast fell and was slain because of love. It's not just an action, it's a directive. You want keys to the kingdom? It starts with love."

We thanked Malcolm as he walked away.

We asked Ezekiel who had come near if he had need of anything. His response was unexpected when he said, "The co-laboring of the sons, in love, is what gave the strength of the matter to bring this about. There are many things on the scroll that will be slain, and the weapon is love."

> *Father, I ask for the Supernatural Love to be given to Ezekiel as he co-labors with our angels and of those that draw near to LifeSpring, for it to be poured out upon them as a directive, as a complete understanding, because it's way beyond what we can think of. It is way beyond what we know.*

[We throw around the word *love* and what that truly means.]

> *Father, we ask that we may co-labor and wield the weapon of love.*
>
> *I also ask for the substance of clarity in this for all, for me, and the truth defender membrane, to be placed upon all of us.*
>
> *Also, the look and see cream so that our eyes may see.*

I ask for the frequency earphones so that we all may hear the frequencies of Heaven and what You are bringing.

Thank You, Father, because I know Your heart is about love, and You showed us that today.

I see what your heart is, about this ministry, and what it's doing because this is Your Kingdom. That's why this enemy has been slain. You told us recently that You come against those that come against Your Kingdom work. Thank You.

The Shofars

Stephanie found herself standing in front of a table with a shofar on it. An interesting looking creature came in, picked up the shofar off the table and begin walking away. Stephanie decided to follow along with him.

She described, "We've come to a place, and I am watching him standing in a row now with all these other beings and angelic hosts. There are also men and women in white and all of them have shofars and trumpets. They haven't blown the trumpets and shofars yet, but they are ready." Stephanie asked the living creature, "May I ask what this is about?

"He turned around to me and he took me to a picture of when the Israelites walked around the wall of Jericho, silently marching around the wall. But on the last day, they blew their shofars and trumpets. This is something that is being similarly done in this realm that we are in. That is why they weren't blowing the shofars yet. There is a directive coming from Heaven which is why they are standing and waiting."

The living creature said, "When the directive comes, the walls will fall down and at the shout of the Lord, at the blowing of the shofars, in Heaven, from Heaven."

Stephanie replied, "It's the same concept as what was done on earth, that day at Jericho. Is this day in relation to this ministry specifically?"

The Elevation

The living creature said, "This is the elevation. With new levels comes new warfare."

Stephanie explained, "Now he's gone back to hearing this directive from Heaven. They are listening. I can't hear what things are being said, but I can tell they're listening."

The angelic being said, "This is help. This is help from the Lord. This is new, it's from a paradigm, from a new place. Because of the elevation, there's extraordinary help."

Stephanie said, "Heaven, I have so many questions about this. Ron, while you were governing from your star by praying in the spirit, it set this up from that paradigm. Where you were governing, this has strategically been put in place."

The angelic being remarked, "This is the work of the Kingdom."

Stephanie commented, "There is such anticipation in the air, and there were all classes and sizes of beings around. I saw this little guy, he was smaller than the rest of them, but it was purposeful, too. Now, it's like I'm being pulled away, but I can see the different dimension or parallel that they're in. Thank you for that, Heaven, for a small teaching on the governing, of the picture of what is taking place from being obedient."

From Heaven we heard, "Obedience is better than sacrifice." Someone speaking from Heaven said, "The reason that there's much praying in the spirit regarding these scrolls is because anything else in your natural mind, you would think you've done it yourselves. This is how you know and can stand in the reality that you are not doing any of this in and of yourselves. These are scrolls from the Lord regarding governing territory that is not *in and of yourselves*. You are completely and totally reliant upon these instructions and praying in the spirit regarding your scrolls."

Stephanie remarked, "That's why when I did my star the other day, Wisdom had me open the door and we could see the angels were already doing the work, because I was obedient and prayed in the spirit regarding my scrolls."

Stephanie asked, "Heaven, is there something Ron needs to do for those to be released to blow the shofar?"

A voice from Heaven replied, "You are on day three of the marching around the wall."

Stephanie remarked, "That means Friday will be day seven. I'm excited! I get the anticipation now. This is so simplistic. The information we've been given has been very simple, and it's just a matter of trusting that what we've done is doing something."

Governing from Within Our Star

We finished that phase of our engagement with Heaven and asked to meet with Lydia. Lydia met us and led us down a hallway to a large, illuminated room. She said, "I want to show you something new."

In the room we entered, it was solid white. Everything was very bright. The room contained no furniture, but one could hear music. There was such an atmosphere of peace. Of course, it would be in Heaven, but this was very specific to something happening in this ministry.

It's as if we saw *a directive of the Senior Advocates* bringing each client into this place, it's like it was pumped full of pristine air. Wondering why were in this room, we called Wisdom alongside.

Wisdom appeared and said, "This is the illumination. It is a picturesque instruction on how to take the first steps to your star work."

Stephanie asked, "Wisdom, how can we give this instruction in words to the people? It is such a simplistic work—the star work, because it is Heaven doing the work. Are we to obey the two or three steps that we've been given?"

She replied, **"The first step** is having Wisdom illuminate the path."

Stephanie remarked, "I do feel the illumination here. I feel it, but I also don't feel myself. All of me has been left behind."

Wisdom continued, **"Govern from rest. It's in the stillness of this place that you will find the way. This is a part of bringing your spirit forward. In this place, you leave your flesh behind."**

Stephanie added, "I feel the stillness here."[88]

Wisdom explained, "From here, you can also receive the instruction of the Lord where you will know how your scrolls will be received by you."

Stephanie remarked, "All of a sudden, I am seeing a door open. When you come into this place, there's stillness and quietness. You've left your flesh behind. Once I was truly at that place of stillness, the door opened in front of me and the path has been illuminated, but it's much brighter. As I take a step, *I feel like I'm walking on*

---

[88] Isaiah 30:15 "For thus says the Lord GOD, the Holy One of Israel: 'In returning and rest you shall be saved; in quietness and confidence shall be your strength.'"

light and it's as if this light is going *through* the star that I'm walking on. I'm seeing this star from within now. I am looking *in* the star. You know how Heaven has taught us to look deeper, but right now, I'm looking at the surface of the full star and that light is going through it. I'm walking *into* it. I've done the initial work, walking into the middle of my star, literally into the middle of it, like sci-fi stuff. When I walked to the middle of the star, I *became* inside of it and I could move my star from inside of it, from in that place.

"This is my place that I govern from. The place that I have deeded over to the Lord, and *I'm inside of it*. From inside of this place, 'Wisdom, what do I do so that knowledge will come?'"

The understanding that we initially governed from above our star is how we started this understanding. Now, we're beginning to understand the **governing from within it**. This is what that's going to look like. Are we putting it (the star) on essentially?"

Stephanie began going over the steps we had just learned. I walked from this lit path that I could feel under my feet into the middle of the star, as if I stepped into it.

"I'm suspended inside of it, but now I see engineering around me. If I move my hand this way (moving her hand forward), I don't know if the star moved or the governing. It is moving with me—because it's above and it's below, it's to the right and left, as well. I can turn, and I can see all this engineering around me—this technology. We will ask for scrolls inside of here."

Wisdom explained, *"It's from in here that you ask for the pathways to the different dimensions.* It's from in this place, you will do dimensional work—paradigm work."

Stephanie replied, "'Wisdom, I can see the different paradigms.' She is going to eventually teach us about the different technologies. I see the insides of clocks around me. I see letters. All of it is suspended around me. I see equations and geometries, I see maps. It's all around. I'm in this very secure place in the middle knowing that this belongs to the Lord. It's from this place that He will teach these secret things."

Wisdom said, "These are paradoxical matters."

Stephanie remarked, "This is truly interesting, Wisdom. I want to say that Ron and I are open to everything Heaven wants to teach us from of this place. May I ask a question? Is this the next step after we rule from our governance? Is this the next step from the place that you've taught us initially? **Is the next step to ask for the illuminated path from that initial room, from that place and from that stillness?** You showed me that what I'm walking on, actual light, goes into the star. Is it correct that *that's* the next step we step in?"

Wisdom replied, "These are the next steps."

Stephanie commented, "You're going to lay out steps for us as we teach this, aren't you?"

Wisdom remarked, "Yes, for the sake of the teaching."

Stephanie explained, "When she said 'teaching,' she showed me the reality of how the Father has placed the ability in each of us to learn differently. Every person is different. But from here, we will all understand the teaching.

"Thank you, Wisdom. It is only from Heaven that we would be given understanding that all minds could understand. Can I stay in here (inside the star)?"

Wisdom replied, "You will eventually be in this place—this seat. This is where you will be learning to rule and reign from. Your star is connected to the Bright and Morning Star and this is how you will rule and reign together."

Stephanie exclaimed, "Well, I'm going to get on this walkway of light, and I am going to come back into this room. I see the door going back through that door.

"By the way, when I originally opened the door, it looked like outer space directly to my star. Now, I'm back in the illuminated room, and Lydia is here. We walked out of the room, and she walked away."

Chapter 28
The Kingdom Dynamics of Our Arche

In this engagement, Stephanie and I were to go to the beach with Malcolm. We walked to and through automatic double doors that opened leaving the Business Complex, and we stepped onto a beach.

Two chairs were on the beach for Stephanie and me, while Malcolm sat on a box facing us. We could see the ocean in front of us. We could hear the waves. We could see the sun and hear the wind and the trees rustling. It was very peaceful. We were told that this was his territory—his landscape.

Malcolm explained, "This is the outer edge of my territory. You are here because you are learning about governing."

We then asked for understanding about *arche* (pronounced *ar-key*[89]). We were pulled back to a bird's eye view and could see us sitting there with him, but there was more of his territory and landscape that we were able to see beyond the immediate view.

We saw a library and the place that he had brought us where the whiteboard is. We could see his house—his mansion, but also see other places in other dimensions. Suddenly, we were back in front of him. We asked, "Malcolm, are these your territories where you rule from and govern?"

Malcolm replied, "It is! Boy, do I wish I would've known about governing when I walked upon the earth. Things would have been much different. My leadership skills would have been much different. *My destiny now is governing from this place.*"

Stephanie noted, "Malcolm, I get the sense that you're teaching us is a sort of governing."

Malcolm answered, "It absolutely is. I have been entrusted by the Father to bring knowledge for the expansion of the Kingdom of God on earth. It has been part of my own redemption.

"The mistakes that I made when I was on earth have been redeemed in Heaven, and now, I am able to help teach.

---

[89] The plural is: archai (pronounced *ar ki* with long i

"It is all about the goodness of the Father. You know the Scripture about how when you're weak, He is strong? When you walk upon the earth, and you are weak, and He is strong. Well here, He's even stronger. My failures there, He has redeemed. It's part of my story. My *destiny* continues forward here."

We asked, "Would this be considered your *arche*?"

Malcolm replied, **"Your *arche* is your place and your position of authority. It is your territory from which you rule from. It is a positional place.**

"When Satan fell, the *arche* that the angels were in, which was their place—their position, they walked away from it. This is an authority. When you realize you are a son, you realize you have a territory and a landscape, and you govern from there."

We asked, "How is this compared to the Stars?"

He replied, "Your *arche*—your realm of authority has *your stars within it*. The stars are just in a dimension of the realm of our authority, the positional place of where we will lead from. *The stars are an entity that we must govern.*

"You, Ron, have four stars—one personal star and three pertaining to LifeSpring that you govern, one of which concerns the finances that you govern. One concerns the people associated with LifeSpring and the other concerns the outlets and expansion of LifeSpring. It is very specific about what we will govern, but it's not the whole package. It's not the only thing we use our authority for, it's just a piece. The vastness that you've been shown, *that* is your positional place. I can't even describe it. It's so large. This is part of that as we learn and maneuver.

We replied to Malcolm, "We want to know this concept for the sake of teaching the people and for the sake of governing correctly. We want the heart of the Father and what He has for us as we learn this and understand this."

He responded, "For instance, as you govern members of your family, and as you learn this, as you walk in this, there is an instant deliverance to come because *that is the heart of the Lord*. That is His heart. His heart is peace and unity and us being able to co-labor with Heaven as these things come to pass in people's lives.

We replied, "Teach us to govern like Jesus taught the disciples. Teach us to govern like Jesus governed. That's what we want."

Malcolm asked, "What season would you say you are in your life?"

Stephanie replied that she was in an interesting season.

Malcolm queried, "What did you learn about patience recently? It's a positional thing, too."

Stephanie, speaking for both of us said, "Malcolm, I just wanted you to know I'm seated back in this chair in front of this ocean. Whatever it takes for me to expand—to get this, I want it. I don't want to be limited."

He replied, "You aren't limited. You are new." He then leaned over and said, "If I was to tell you everything right now, you couldn't handle it. Your body couldn't handle it. Trust the process."

I remarked, "We *are* getting it 'line upon line, precept upon precept, here a little there a little....'"

"Well, we say 'yes' to Heaven. We don't want to be limited. Whatever it is that we need to be taught, we ask for the grace for eyes to see and ears to hear."

Malcolm exclaimed, "Now you're governing!"

Governing is submission.

It's such a submissive process.

Malcolm was finished with the lesson, so we got up and walked back inside the building—the LifeSpring Business Complex.

Chapter 29
The Kingdom Dynamics of Freedom from Religion

This engagement started out very differently. Stephanie heard the phrase "Foundational Principles of Life" coming from a man in white she had never seen before. When asked his name, he told us it was Mark. He looked very similar to the guy that plays Jesus in *The Chosen*. The only difference is his hair is lighter.

Stephanie greeted him and asked, "Hi, Mark. What is it you want to teach us today?"

Mark reached under a high-top desk he was standing near and pulled out a Menorah with candles. He set it on the desk and began lighting each with a flame. Stephanie noticed that he had a Jewish star on his jacket.

Mark stated, "He brought me through the fire."

Stephanie asked, "Are you one of those who was in a concentration camp?"

He replied, "This is martyrdom. He was with me through the fire."

Stephanie explained, "Mark then took me to a table that felt like a table prepared in the presence of my enemies. He set up bread and oil, sat down and began eating the bread dipped in oil."

We were seated at the table with Mark, where he has been dipping bread in oil and a lampstand came up behind him. I asked Mark if he was introduced to Yeshua or if Yeshua introduced Himself to him before he died. He said Yeshua had done that to many of them, and that's why He was there with him *through the fire*—letting him know that he is a son, and that He had established this territory, this place for His son. He said, "He's calling His sons to govern. That's the beckoning of Yeshua. He is calling His sons to step into their territory and their landscape and to govern. That's going to bring 'His Kingdom come, and His will be done.'"

Mark then opened a portal—a door from the room we were originally in, and we could see his territory and his landscape. Stephanie remarked, "A lot of what I was experiencing or feeling was that we humans still make judgments upon who Jesus and the Father decides to save. This is a lesson in that, because he showed me a hologram of many Jewish people. I could see the stars on their jackets, but they were in a paradigm, ruling from their territory. It's a lesson for many, especially in regards to who do we think we are, making absolutes on behalf of people who were there and died, yet we had believed they didn't go to Heaven because we thought they didn't know Yeshua? Not true. Yeshua ushered in many in the Holocaust. Who are we to make that determination?

"They essentially did receive Him. They received His provision. They just didn't know the four spiritual laws and our little Romans Road and stuff.

She continued, "I don't know why this was necessary for us to hear today, but I'm struck by the entire matter that it's about the religious spirit. Who are we to judge? What's so interesting is he gave me that picture of Shadrack, Meshack and Abednego. Mark experienced the same thing, but he kept saying that Yeshua was there with him through the fire and got him through the fire, and then he was instantly in his very own territory. I know this is a piece to a puzzle for later. I know that it is."

Lydia had appeared and spoke up, "The remarkability of this message will shake some to their core. The religious spirit raises its ugly head."

Stephanie asked Lydia, "It there anything else that you want me to ask or say about this particular message?"

Lydia replied, "There is more to come," and she smiled.

We thanked her and then heard the word 'mandate.'

Lydia remarked, "The mandate is about *The Foundational Principles of Life*—understand it as a mandate and as a principle.

---

*Sons cannot walk freely
bound by a religious spirit.*

"Territorial and landscape privileges are for those who lay that down. The King is waiting on the other side of the veil for those who have been blinded by the religious spirits."

Stephanie commented, "Lydia, we have a prayer paradigm for those regarding the religious spirit, and it is very powerful. It set me free on many levels. Is this a mandate to be part of the reading before people have sessions?"

Stephanie noted, "I got a green light on that one—like a literal light came on."

Stephanie asked me, "What are your thoughts about having that be one of the reading materials?"

She was referring to a court scenario we have regarding *Divorcing the Religious Spirit* we have as a blog post. We have it here on the next page:

Divorcing the Spirit of Religion

This information is based upon our engagement in the realms of Heaven while at our "Engaging the Glory Conference" gathering in Wilmington, NC, August 2021.

Many have found themselves bound by the spirit of religion of different flavors. Protestants have a different flavor from Catholics, Pentecostals from Baptists, Jews from other forms, and interestingly, you did not have to have a church background to become religious. You may have been raised with no input from organized religion, yet still be entrapped by the spirit of religion.

Often, we find a hidden nuptial is part of the package. With or without your consent, many of us were married to a church or denomination. You may never have known about it, but it nevertheless occurred. Many of the vows, covenants, oaths, or recitations we made created these nuptials to the spirit of religion, but since the spirit of religion is a very wicked bedfellow, we want to be free of this marriage to religion. It hinders the forward movement in our life and must be dealt with if we are to be able to govern our territories and the landscapes Heaven has for us as sons. We will deal with those nuptials in the court session you are about to embark upon.

Think of the part of your life dealing with religion as a territory. You were designed with your spirit engaging with spiritual things. However, most of us only engaged spiritual or religious matters from the realm of our soul, and somewhere in the process, the evil spirit of religion became involved. Earmarks of the spirit of religion are:

- Pride
- Arrogance
- Self-exaltation
- Restricting access to the Kingdom of Heaven
    - We have lots of rules and regulations to follow to be "good enough" to associate with us
    - We are always about bondage—never freedom
- Long and powerless prayers and rituals
- Protectiveness over what we believe to the point of murderous acts or words
- Insular activities toward others
- Expectations and demands that others agree with our version of religion
- Condemning of others
- Prone to backbiting, gossip, jealousy, and offense
- Majoring on minors
- Rigid interpretation of Scripture
- Want to look 'holy' and 'spiritual' but inwardly are dead and ugly
- Despise who you cannot control

These are not *all* the earmarks of a spirit of religion, but they are common ones. Aren't you ready to be free of every vestige of religion?

Following are guidelines for a court case for divorce from the spirit of religion. Read through it first, so you know what you are about to do, then engage your spirit, allow your soul to sit back, then re-read it aloud as a court case you are presenting to the Father—the Just Judge.

Prayer Template

Father, I first request access to the realms of Heaven. I request access to the Court of Divorce, in the name of Jesus Christ.

I request the exposure of every hidden nuptial regarding the spirit of religion or any religious entity, made by me or any of my bloodline ancestors, all the way back to the hand of the Father, whether made knowingly or unknowingly, with which I am entangled.

[If you discover more than one hidden nuptial, go through them one by one using the following portion of this court scenario.]

I am requesting an absolute divorce from the spirit of religion. This marriage was not entered into willingly by me or with full knowledge of all such a marriage entailed.

I also request a Certificate of Divorce regarding this nuptial, in the name of Jesus Christ of Nazareth.

I testify that it is the desire of my heart to be free of the spirit of religion. Where I (or any of my bloodline ancestors) have willingly participated with the spirit of religion in any form, and any time, or in any fashion, I repent. I ask Your forgiveness. I forgive those who coerced me or my ancestry into this union.

I repent for the embrace and participation by me or my bloodline in religious rituals.

I repent for all (including myself) who bowed the knee in worship of any deity, person, or image.

I repent for having a form of godliness but denying the power of God.

I repent for every limitation of You, Father, Your Son Jesus, or the Holy Spirit or any You used to fulfill the purposes of God in our lives.

I repent for putting other gods before You, whether done by me or any of my ancestors.

I repent for every trade made with religion and religious institutions, whether made by me or my bloodline.

I repent for yielding to the spirit of religion in any fashion, whether by me or my ancestry.

I repent for the embrace of fear regarding religion in any fashion, at any time, by anyone in my bloodline or myself.

I confess these things as sin. I repent on my and their behalf, and I ask the Blood of Jesus to cover them and every ramification and impact of them, in Jesus' name. I forgive, bless, and release them.

I repent on behalf of those who initiated this in my generations and for those who perpetuated it, and in so doing, hindered us from true relationship with You, Father.

I request that the territory of my heart that is ruled by this spirit of religion and impacts my mind, my thoughts, my actions, and my movement be deeded to You, Lord of Hosts.

I request angels be sent to sweep up all debris left by the spirit of religion or those in concert with the spirit of religion, in Jesus' name.

I request that the timeline of my life and that of my generations be restored to the timing of Heaven for my life and my generations, in Jesus' name.

I am requesting these things in the name of Jesus, the Firstborn Son of the Living God.

Await the Verdict

Watch, sense, or hear what is being done in the court:

- Wait will the paperwork is being completed.
- Watch to see your name on the paperwork.
- Watch for the Judge's stamp upon them.

- Hand the Title Deed to the territory of your heart owned by the spirit of religion over the attendant in the Court.
- Receive a copy of the new Title Deed with the Lord of Hosts as the new owner.
- Receive the Certificate of Divorce
- Follow any instructions related to any reclamation work to be done.
- Prophetically remove the wedding band and the shackles from your life.
- Rejoice in your freedom.

———·———

Chapter 30
Living Kingdom Dynamics

As we engaged Heaven, we noted a lot of fanfare in Heaven, and Stephanie was hearing the lyrics to the song, "Here comes the glory of the Lord, sweeping in the room."

We asked, "Why is there a lot of fanfare in Heaven?"

Malcolm replied, "Because the sons are taking *ownership in their sonship*. There *is* something to be said about *owning* your sonship. It is a mindset of cooperation. It's a belief in your sonship apart from your soul and your flesh. It is a cooperating with the glory. It is a cooperating with trusting. It's a cooperation with believing. It will become a condition of the heart to walk in these paradigms—these dimensional and quantum paradigms.

"There is something to be said about not understanding from your natural minds the quantum leaping that you experience when you step into Heaven. Wrapping your head around it will not be an issue.

"This is a trusted, positional way the sons will walk. You've heard the phrase, 'Your steps upon the earth.' There *is* a vibration to the steps in quantum leaping. Your steps will be felt, they will be heard. It is a rulership—these steps, and it *is* dynamic."

Stephanie remarked, "I just said in my heart, 'Is this where Enoch walked?'"

Malcolm said, "Absolutely. This is where King David walked, but the King always knew he was a son."

Stephanie commented, "Malcolm just showed me a type of graduation from one realm to the next, and that's what it will feel like."

"You're talking about a heavenly realm aren't you, Malcolm?" she asked.

Malcolm said, "Well, we are learning about quantum leaping. These are those glory-to-glory moments that were talked about in the Word. You have always thought about it as a very flat plane. Dimensional thinking is not flat. Glory-to-glory is a leap. Realm-to-realm is a leap. Trans-dimensional thinking will become a norm. Its revelation of heightened sensitivity will become how the sons walk on the earth, because they will be walking trans-dimensionally in the spirit."

Stephanie, "Well, Malcolm, that's exciting to know. You are showing me that *is* the glory. There is that song again, 'Here comes the glory of the Lord, sweeping in the room.'"

Malcolm said, "This is beyond the favor of the Lord. That is why the cry from Heaven has been 'relational.' Relational is all about trust."

Stephanie replied, "Malcolm, is that why you've taught us about the consequential lien work, because it opens up the *trust* of heaven, which is our inheritance, that *this is* our inheritance, this quantum leaping information and dynamics?"

Malcolm responded, "Yes. Relational. The Father is removing the barriers that have kept his sons from being in *full* relationship with Him.

"The severity of the crimes against His sons, from the enemy, has not gone unnoticed. There is great vindication for the sons in this. The levels in which they will walk have already trampled underfoot the enemy. Imagine the trampling that will occur in future days as His sons come into the full understanding and knowledge and walk *from* these heavenly places—these quantum leaps. The truth of the matter is, there is no way the gates of hell can prevail against them, which is why there has been 'the lie' down the ages in the church from the pulpits that you are not worthy to be His sons.

"Talk about a shaking—there is a major shaking in the spirit as the kingdom of darkness realizes and understands they cannot stop this. It's here. That's why when they push, you *DO* push back. That's why you *press in* because you *will* walk in the fullness of this."

Our engagements for this volume of Kingdom Dynamics were ending with the reminders from Malcolm and others about living out our sonship. Remember what was said,

The sons must know they are sons in order to son.

Let's be about our Father's business.

———·———

Appendix A

The Kingdom Dynamic of Accessing the Realms of Heaven

A tremendous privilege we share in this time in history is the ability to access the realms of Heaven with ease. Many of us were taught that Heaven is only for after you die. Heaven is much more than a final destination on a journey but also can be a vital aspect of that journey.

What I am about to share is vital in progressing in the various Courts of Heaven. We can access the Mercy Court in the Heavenly realm while fully planted here on the earth, but to maximize our endeavors in the Courts of Heaven, we need to learn how to operate FROM Heaven.

In teaching on accessing the realms of Heaven, I often point out some simple facts. If you were to tell me you were a citizen of a particular town, but you could tell me little of it from your personal experience, I would have a tendency to doubt the authenticity of your citizenship. I am a citizen of a small town in central North Carolina. I am familiar with the location of the city hall, police station, hospital, local county courthouse, Sheriff's Department, and much more. I know where many sporting events will be held. I know where the parks are. I know many of the stores and restaurants. I am familiar with this small town. Yet, if I were to ask the average believer what they can describe of Heaven from personal experience, the answer will likely be nothing. They have no personal experience of Heaven that they can relate to me. It does not have to be like that.

In Matthew 3, Jesus informed us that the Kingdom of Heaven was at hand. You could say, "The Kingdom of Heaven is as close as your hand." Hold your hand up in front of your nose as close as you could. Do not touch your nose. Heaven is closer to you than that. It is not far, far away up in the sky. It is not "over yonder" as some old hymns describe. It is a very present reality separated from us by a very thin membrane—and we can access it by faith. It is very simple.

When Jesus was baptized in the River Jordan, as He came up out of the water IMMEDIATELY the heavens were opened. He both saw (a dove) and heard (a voice coming from Heaven). This one act of Jesus restored our ability to access Heaven. We can experience open heavens over our life. We don't have to wait. We can live conscious of the realm of Heaven and live out of that reality!

Everything we do as believers we must do by faith.

Accessing the realms of Heaven is done the same way. Prophetic acts can create realities for us. It is the same with this. You can visualize stepping from one room into another easily. It is like stepping from one place to another. To learn to access the realms of Heaven, you will follow the same pattern.

Stand up from where you are now and prepare to work with me. You can experience the realms of Heaven right now! You don't have to wait until you are dressed up in a long box at the local funeral home or decorating an urn. You can experience Heaven while you are alive! Remember, we enter the Kingdom as a child.

Quiet yourself down. Turn off distracting background noises if possible. Prepare to relax and focus. Now, say this with me:

> *Father, I would like to access the realms of Heaven today, so right now, by faith, I take a step into the realms of Heaven. [As you say that, take a step forward.] Imagine you are going from one place to another in a single step. Once you have done so, pay attention to what you see and hear. You may see very bright lights; you may see a river, a pastoral scene, a garden—any number of*

things. Right now, you are experiencing a taste of Heaven. You will notice the peace that pervades the atmosphere of Heaven. You might notice the air seems electric with life. The testimonies I've heard are always amazing and beautiful to hear.

Now spend a few minutes in this place. Remember, Jesus said that to enter the Kingdom you must come as a little child. I often coach people to imagine yourself as an 8-year-old with what you are seeing. What would an 8-year-old do? He or she would be inquisitive and ask, "What is this? What does that do? Where does that go? Can I go here?" If a child saw a river or a lake, what would that child want to do? Most would want to jump in the water.

The variety is infinite. The colors—amazing! The sounds are so beautiful. You can learn to do this on a regular basis. When you access the realms of Heaven, you are home. You were made to experience the beauty that is Heaven.

> *The reason learning to access the realms of Heaven is crucial to engaging the Courts of Heaven is that much of what we do is done FROM Heaven. We need to learn to engage Heaven and work from it.*

Many people tell me they can't "see" visually in the spirit. Often, they are discounting the ability they do have. They may be discounting their "knower." Every believer has a "knower" at work within them. This "knower" who is Holy Spirit at work within you helps you perceive things. Whether something is good or evil, He works to guide you more than you may have realized. Most navies that have submarines have a device known as sonar. Sonar gives a submarine "eyes" to see what is in their vicinity. They can detect what the object is by the ping emitted by the sonar. They can determine the distance to the object and if it is another submarine. They can even identify what class of submarine it might be. Sonar is invaluable in this setting, but a video camera would be rather useless underwater.

The military has a similar device for above ground situations known as radar. It functions in much the same manner. If a pilot were flying through thick cloud cover, the pilot would need to know what is in his path. Radar becomes his eyes.

Some people function visually. They often see what amounts to pictures or video images when they "see" in the spirit. They may see more detail. Yet one operating by his or her "knower" (their spiritual radar or sonar) can be just as effective as a seer. If you operate more like sonar or radar, don't discount what you "see" in that manner. It is how I function, and I have been doing this type of work for many years.

I can often detect where an angel is in the room (or if it is one of the men or women in white linen and not an angel). I can often detect how many are present and whether they have something they are to give to someone. I can detect any number of things and even though it is not "visual." it is still "seeing." It will set your mind at ease when you understand that operating by your knower is just as valid as any other type of vision. It will help you to realize you have been seeing much more than you know and you may know much more than some who only see.

———·———

References

Strong, J. (n.d.). *Strong's Concordance.*

Description

Heaven is vitally interested in seeing its sons step into who they really are. Where religion has told us who we are not, Heaven is telling us that we are overcomers in this world and the next.

This book covers a variety of Kingdom Dynamics that need to be active in our lives. These dynamics will shake cities as the sons arise and embrace their sonship. You can live your life without hope or with the Hope of Glory—Jesus arising in your being. Choose the latter!

About the Author

Dr. Ron Horner is an apostolic teacher specializing in the Courts of Heaven. He has written over a twenty books on the Courts of Heaven, engaging Heaven, working with angels, or living from revelation.

He currently trains people in engaging the Courts of Heaven in a weekly online teaching session. You can register to participate and discover more about the Courts of Heaven prayer paradigm on his various websites, classes, products, and services found here:

www.ronhorner.com

Other Books by Dr. Ron M. Horner

Building Your Business from Heaven Down

Building Your Business from Heaven Down 2.0

Commissioning Angels – Volume 1

Cooperating with The Glory

Courts of Heaven Process Charts

Dealing with Trusts & Consequential Liens

Engaging Angels in the Realms of Heaven

Engaging Heaven for Revelation – Volume 1

Engaging Heaven for Revelation – Volume 2

Engaging Heaven for Trade

Engaging the Courts for Ownership & Order

Engaging the Courts for Your City (*Paperback, Leader's Guide & Workbook*)

Engaging the Courts of Healing & the Healing Garden

Engaging the Courts of Heaven

Engaging the Help Desk of the Courts of Heaven

Engaging the Mercy Court of Heaven

Four Keys to Dismantling Accusations

Freedom from Mithraism

Let's Get it Right!

Lingering Human Spirits

Lingering Human Spirits – Volume 2

Living Spirit Forward

Overcoming the False Verdicts of Freemasonry

Overcoming Verdicts from the Courts of Hell

Releasing Bonds from the Courts of Heaven

Unlocking Spiritual Seeing

SPANISH

Cómo Proceder en la Corte Celestial de Misericordia

Las Cuatro Llaves para Anular las Acusaciones

Liberando Bonos en las Cortes Celestiales

Liberando Su Visión Espiritual

Sea Libre del Mitraísmo

Tablas de Proceso de la Cortes del Cielo

Viviendo desde el Espíritu

www.ingramcontent.com/pod-product-compliance
Lightning Source LLC
Chambersburg PA
CBHW022000160426
43197CB00007B/210